SEEDS OF ADVICE
To Sail Through Hard Times

Lessons from Bhagavad Gita &
Modern Behavioral Science
To Solve Life's Problems And
Enhance Self Awareness

VIKRAM KHAITAN

Pledge

I pledge in the name of my ishta-devata Shri Krishna that the net earnings from the sales of this book shall be utilized solely for the purpose of helping the humankind through charity, irrespective of their race, color, religion, caste, gender or abilities.

-Vikram Khaitan

PUBLISHED BY:
VIKRAM KHAITAN
(vikram.khaitan@gmail.com)

ASIN: B099THCW5M
ISBN-13: 979-8540346535

SECOND EDITION

COPYRIGHT © Vikram Khaitan 2021
All rights reserved. No parts of this publication may be reproduced, stored, retrieved, printed, and transmitted, in any form or by any means, electronic, mechanical, photocopying, recording, or otherwise, without the express prior permission of the author.

TABLE OF CONTENTS

ABOUT THE BOOK VI
WHY SECOND EDITION? VII
FOREWORD VIII
BASIS OF CRITIC'S REVIEW X
FOREWORD XII
ACCOLADES & READERS' REVIEWS XVI
INTRODUCTION 1
CHAPTER 1: CALMNESS FOR ANGER 13
CHAPTER 2: MODESTY FOR ARROGANCE 19
CHAPTER 3: REPUGNANCE TO LUST 27
CHAPTER 4: ALTRUISM OVER GREED 36
CHAPTER 5: CLARITY OVER BEWILDERMENT 40
CHAPTER 6: CHEER OVER JEALOUSY 45
CHAPTER 7: SOLACE AFTER GRIEF 52
CHAPTER 8: FORTITUDE AGAINST FEAR 58
CHAPTER 10: EQUALITY OVER DISCRIMINATION 75
CHAPTER 11: ZEAL OVER LAZINESS 80
CHAPTER 12: CAMARDERIE BEATS LONELINESS 87
CHAPTER 14: RESISTANCE TO TEMPTATION 106
CHAPTER 15: CHASTITY FROM SINFULNESS 116
CHAPTER 16: HARNESS THE WANDERING MIND 124
CHAPTER 17: THE VIRTUE OF FORGIVENESS 131
CHAPTER 18: SEEKING PEACE 137
CHAPTER 19: DEVELOP SELF AWARENESS – THE CONCLUSION 144
ONE MOMENT PLEASE 158
GRATITUDE 159
ABOUT THE AUTHOR 160
DISCLAIMER 161
THEY SAID IT! 162
REFERENCES 170

ABOUT THE BOOK

Are you overwhelmed by the problems and chaos in your Life, Career, or Relationships? Do you want to understand how to sort your life, deal with your inner vices like lust, anger, ego, greed, grief, jealousy, and succeed in whatever you apply your mind into?

If the answer is yes! Then read on ahead...

Here is a perfect set of solutions if you want to successfully, navigate through hardships, subdue the chaos to grow as a person, and achieve your goals!

This book will help you train your mind to develop the strength of healthy intelligence and enable you to deal with all situations.

Are you ready to take charge of your life and shape your own destiny? Become more positive, act creatively, generate exceptional ideas at will, solve problems wisely, & stand apart from the crowd.

You can awaken your inner self conscience and become a superior human being. Like the smartest of thinkers, you too can transform the way you think and predict the future.

For most people, attaining peace and self-awareness from within remains a challenge for as long as a lifetime, because they look for happiness outside themselves. This book will show you the path of introspection to look inwards and discover the best person in the world, which is YOU!

Why Second Edition?

The first edition of this book published in July 2021 has received immense love and thundering response from the readers. It seemed necessary to bring forth and exhibt their opinions about the first edition of this book.

This book has won a critic's acclaim and a foreword by Mr.Ashish Mukherjee of Kolkata, West Bengal. He is a Chartered Engineer, Valuer, Books and Films critic, Co-founder of Ananda Bazar Partika, Yoga Exponent, Founder of Knowledge Hub and GCM.

Mr.Mukherjee has awarded his highest ever rating of 9.4/10 till this print and the basis of his rating is also explained herein. Resultantly, the book has found its way to the window display at the prestegious British Chamber Council Library, 91 Camac Street, Kolkata.

Dr.K.R.S.Nair has also written a foreword for this book. He is a veteran exponent of the Bhagavad Gita, an ex-banker, Amazon #1 bestselling author of 4 titles, Corporate Trainer specialized in behavioral science, winner of ten awards (national and international), and has authored 100+ articles. As a reader, the minutest of details could not escape the hawk eyes of Dr.Nair, hence several corrective suggestions that were felt necessary have been incorporated in this edition.

Shri.Vijay Rupani ji, Hon'ble Chief Minister of Gujarat has written a letter of appreciation for this book. Also, some of the readers' review are published in this edition.

The main contents of this second edition is the same as the first edition.

FOREWORD

karmajaṁ buddhiyuktā hi phalaṁ tyaktvā manīṣiṇaḥ|
janmabandhavinirmuktāḥ padaṁ
gacchantyanāmayam || 2-51

The wise, possessed of knowledge, having abandoned the fruits of their actions, and being freed from the fetters of birth, go to the place which is beyond all evil.

For ages now, this belief about the soul has reigned supreme for believers and practitioners of humanity. Though, it is an extract from the Bhagavad Gita, it does not hold true for any singular sect of believers but for the mankind as a whole.

Today, when the world is in a reflective mode, trying to find solutions to the various vices that have smitten humanity, the lessons from Bhagavad Gita serves as an apt guide to pull out humanity from the morass of moral and ethical evil.

The Bhagavad Gita is no religious text. It is rather a dramatic rendition of life lessons which is applicable in all ages. There is no religious discourse or propagation of any particular faith. It is merely the eternal lessons conveyed by the divine to the mortal.

In this book, author Vikram Khaitan has very creatively used these vibrant lessons to address the vices that plague humanity throughout generations. It is important not only to recognize the vices but also understand and adopt the measures to overcome them. The contextual usage of the pragmatic sermons of Gita and the methods laid out to guide people to apply them in an effort to exorcise the buried evil in the mind is an extraordinary effort made by this versatile writer.

Even a veteran like me has been thoroughly impacted by the lessons which have been working life a "Sudarshan Chakra" to eliminate the fallacies from my persona. I feel that this book is a necessity for people to adopt a healthy and chaste lifestyle.

Not only is it a recommendation from my side but an eager appeal to everyone to read and use the learnings from this book to cleanse our society from the predominant turpitude that have been brought about by nefarious human thinking.

Ashis Mukherjee

Chartered Engineer | Valuer | Books and Films critic | Co-founder of Ananda Bazar Partika | Yoga Exponent | Founder of Knowledge Hub and GCM

Kolkata, West Bengal, India

"Seeds of Advice – To Sail Through Hard Times is a unique book in itself helping people to know in-depth about various negativities they are confronting with. In addition, there is wisdom from one of the most scientific ancient books, Bhagavad Gita and various practical ways of overcoming all those negativities.

The author has beautifully explained in simple words but effectively, covering various negative aspects of human beings during modern times commencing from anger to arrogance, lust, greed, confusion, jealousy, grief, fear, depression, discrimination, laziness, loneliness, desperation, temptation, sinfulness and wandering of the mind. In addition, the last three chapters cover important virtues of forgiveness, peace and self-awareness.

In my opinion, this book would prove to be a milestone for humankind. It is a complete guide to help human beings overcoming various negative aspects of life and living peacefully."

Indian Intellectual – 5 out of 5 stars
(Reviewed in India on August 31, 2021)

A book for all seasons with all good reasons.
"An excellent fusion of the past and present to overcome life challenges. The book is very methodical in its approach to addressing human vices. Each chapter covers one problem, goes deep into the reasons, connects with the mythology, and offers the solution to overcome it. I haven't come across many books which connect the diverse era's so magnificently. The writing style has a certain flair to it that keeps you hooked. The best part is each segment is complete in itself, so if you are hard-pressed for time, just read the topic which attracts you the most or in another way, the problem which is troubling you the most and move on."

S.D.Kar – 5 out of 5 stars
(Reviewed in India on September 4, 2021)

Must Read
"I would recommend this book to everyone who wanted to read indian scriptures but never had it

Basis of Critic's Review

Letter ref: KH-023/OY67 dtd. 24.09.2021 from Mr.Ashish Mukherjee, Books and Films Critic, is reproduced here-under as the basis for his review and awarding his best rating of 9.4/10

This is a general certification for the book "Seeds of Advice" – To Sail Through Hard Times by author Vikram Khaitan. The assessment of the book has been done based on the following points:

1. **General Look of the book including the cover**: The general lookout of the book including the "Sudarshan Chakra" eliminating all the evils, symbolizes the contents of this book to precision.

2. **The Subject**: The subject is apt as per the present plight of humans who are looking for solutions to grow out of inherent weaknesses and fallacies.

3. **Content**: The content of the book is seamless and to the point with proper emphasis on solutions and control.

4. **Language**: The language is lucid and easy to understand and interpret. It is easy to go through the text and absorb all the messages with ease.

5. **Flow**: The contextual and content flow, both are appropriate and adequate. The reader never gets bored, misled, confused or overwhelmed.

6. **Context**: The author has never deviated from the context and has kept the focus binding on the subject throughout the book. No parenthesis or parallel syntaxing has been used to create unnecessary images.

7. **Clarity of thought**: The author is very clear with his thoughts on the subject and has portrayed the same without ambiguity. He has

formed up his content very well to lay emphatic claim over over the context.

8. **Research**: The author has done good research with the verses of the Bhagavad Gita and used the apt verse at every appropriate conjunction. He has also selected proper quotes and poems to lay emphasis over his observations and statements.

9. **Audience**: The book is universal and not for any selected audience and so is fit to be read by all ages.

10. **Originality**: The creation is a blend of authentic thought, innovative fusion and thoughtful processing of old learnings by the author.

Ashis Mukherjee

FOREWORD

Bhagavad Gita, the 'Lord's Song', originated in the backdrop of a brief episode in the longest epic of the world, *Mahabharata*. Lord Krishna in it symbolizes God, who is the divine Self within all human beings. That is the reason why in the Indian teachings, Self-realization is projected as the real and ultimate goal of all humans, irrespective of their religions. As Swami Kriyananda said in *The Essence of the Bhagavad Gita,* Self-realization and knowledge of God are synonymous. To know one's inner self is to know God. To know the self within is to know everything, but there is a catch. Self-realization is not attained by all. Our sense organs are all outward-bound and receive their inputs only from the external world. The indwelling Self is beyond their comprehension. To reach it, one has to have a very rare endowment. Sankaracharya succinctly put it thus in *Vivekachudamani*:

"Dhurlabham thrayamevaitat
devanugrahahethukam
Manushyathvam, mumukshuathvam,
mahapurushasamsraya:" (V.3)

Only very rarely, thanks to the blessings of God, one attains humaneness, with the godly nature instead of demonic attributes, intense desire for deliverance, and proximity to and guidance of a Satguru.

Kattopanishad (Katha-Upanishad) exhorts *'Utthishtata, jagrata, Prapyavaraan nibhodhata'* (3.14). Here also, while asking the ignorant and deluded people to arise and awake, the scripture is underscoring the need to approach Satgurus to learn how to pursue the desired end. Bhagavad Gita is the essence of Upanishads. The Gita also has a more direct relationship with the Katha Upanishad.

The famous symbols of the chariot, horse, charioteer, rein, etc. have been borrowed into it from this Upanishad. Fire is produced by the attrition of the wood of *the Shami* tree (that contains *Agni* or splendor) during *Yaga* (sacrificial ritual). Likewise, from the splendorous wood called the Katha, the light that is Gita was produced. For instance, see the verse, ibid (3.14). It reverberates in the Indian heart so strongly and everlastingly (and for that matter, it also constitutes the spiritual pride of ancient India). Of all the Upanishads, the Katha Upanishad was the most favorite one for Swami Vivekananda (just as the Eeshavasya was to Mahatma Gandhi) and among all the messages of the scriptures, this one was closest to his heart (Complete Works, Vol. III, pp.318-321).

Bhagavad Gita gives an exhaustive explanation to the above verse in the Katha. It tells you how to 'arise' (*utthishata*) and how to be 'awakened' (*jagrata*). This book *'Seeds of Advice to Sail through Hard Times'* is a lucid exposition of the Gita and focuses on gaining self-awareness and traversing therefrom to self-awakening to become an enlightened human being. "To write well", said Aristotle, "express yourself like the common people, but think like a wise man". In this book, Vikram Khaitan shows both these attributes in abundant measure.

The profound truths about self-awareness and self-awakening are brought out with extreme simplicity, imbued with anecdotes and personal experiences of the author. Here, he artfully brings the ancient teachings of eternal truth into the light of modern understanding, which makes it distinct. While explaining and elaborating the concepts and constructs in the epic, the teachings are juxtaposed with the findings of behavioral scientists to buttress the points convincingly.

For instance, modern behavioral science identifies four unique human endowments, viz., self-awareness, conscience, imagination, and independent will that, if exercised well, will help live a fulfilling life. One can see that in this book the author, with remarkable dexterity, has dovetailed the revelations in the Gita with the conclusions of behavioral scientists in such a manner that ordinary people can sail through the travails of life seamlessly.

Another distinct feature that makes this volume stand apart is the way it has been compiled. Unlike most of the interpretations and studies on the Gita, which, by and large, examine the holy text chapter by chapter and verse by verse, this book takes a different route. The focus here is on the various vices (demonic nature) of people, their classifications, and the various modern means to pre-empt them in the light of the wisdom contained in the 'Lord's Song'. The chapters, albeit numbered as in the Gita, the similarity between the two ends there. The themes in individual chapters are not akin to the Gita. At the same time, every chapter has three to four or five verses from the scripture, cited, analyzed, and the relevant nuggets of wisdom churned out. This is not an easy task to perform. For, it calls for an in-depth study and reflection of the whole of Gita to cull out the contextual verses scattered across the whole text and bring them to one place, under the same chapter. Hats off to the author for this stupendous task ably accomplished.

In this context, I'm reminded of the following verse from the *Gita Dhyanam:*

Sarvopanishado gavo dogdha gopalanandana:
Parttho vatsa sudheerbhokta dugdham
geethamrutham mahat (4)

'All the Upanishads are the cows, the milker is Krishna –the cowherd boy, Partha is the calf, men of purified intellect are the drinkers, the milk is the supreme nectar of the Gita'.

The universal cowherd boy, Lord Krishna, has milked the Upanishads and collected the supreme nectar called the Gita for the men of pure conscience and intellect to drink. Also, through this book, the author has done a yeoman's service to churn out that invaluable, most nutritious, and life-enriching milk in a manner that it got converted into a digestible form, even for men of less pure intellect to drink and become self-awakened.

I'm happy to discern that this remarkable interpretation and transmission of eternal wisdom across the ages will prove an invaluable guide to provide deep insights into the inner self, consciousness, and self-awakening. Not only to sail through hard times but for all times. To live a meaningful, fulfilled, and self-actualizing life. Through this book, Vikram Khaitan has exemplified the Aristotelian concept of expressing like the common people and thinking as a wise man.

I'm happy to have penned a Foreword for this eminently user-friendly title and wish the book and its author Godspeed in the journey forward.

Dr. K. R. S. Nair

Amazon bestselling author of 4 books | Behavioural Science Specialist & Corporate Trainer

keyares51@gmail.com
website: www.krsnair.com

ACCOLADES & READERS' REVIEWS

Letter from Shri.Vijay Rupani ji, Hon'ble Chief Minister of Gujarat State, India

Vijay Rupani
Chief Minister, Gujarat State

Apro/Jnv/2021/08/13/vj

Dt. 13-08-2021

Snehi Shree Vikram ji,
Namaskar.

I am very much thankful to you for forwarding me your book, on **"Seeds of Advice"** self awakening and spiritualizing based on **Shree Bhagavad Gita**.

I congratulate you for becoming bestseller in abroad within short span of time. I appreciate your endeavor to deal with problems by learning specific lessons from Shree Bhagwad Geeta. I am sure that this book will be helpful among devotees to prepare their mind to fight against their inner conflict and lead to the path of self awakening and spirituality. My best wishes to you for your bright future ahead.

(Vijay Rupani)

To,
Shree Vikram Khaitan,

Dr. Ravindra Dey – 5 out of 5 stars
(Reviewed in India on July 23, 2021)

Enlightened

"Vikram this is one more masterpiece from your side. I always had been inspired by our heritage and mythology. Bhagavad Gita teaches us so many things. You have brought out so nicely all the learnings we can have from Bhagavad Gita. I am already experiencing rich benefits in terms of how to manage Anger and Arrogance. Would read at least 2-3 times to take advantage of your masterpiece. Waiting for many more of such works which are so important for mankind and peace."

Dr. KRS Nair – 5 out of 5 stars
(Reviewed in the United States on July 30, 2021)

Self-awakening through self-awareness:
A contemporary study of Bhagavad Gita
"Human beings have both divine and demoniac qualities. The predominant attributes describe you as godly or devilish. Having been blessed with a human life, our endeavor should be to develop self-awareness, the unique human endowment, so that we become self-awakened to lead a fulfilling life. This book gives a brilliant description of the 26 virtues to be cultivated to enhance self-awareness and elaborates 19 vices that should be shunned, to be a fully self-awakened person, drawing attention to the nuggets of wisdom from Bhagavad Gita juxtaposed with appropriate behavioral science inputs. It underscores the need to have a competent Guru to guide properly in this pursuit for excellence in life. A commendable and enlightening creative work."

Vishal Gupta – 5 out of 5 stars
(Reviewed in the United States on July 30, 2021)

Simply Superb!
"This book takes inspiration from one of the greatest books produced by mankind-the Bhagavad Gita. The author has beautifully interpreted this book with regards to important aspects of life. I enjoyed every word, every page. A must-buy!"

Dinesh K Nagpal – 5 out of 5 stars
(Reviewed in India on August 16, 2021)

A practical book to help overcoming various negativities of life simplified this way. It needs to get translated in vernacular languages so that more and more people can read it."

INTRODUCTION

Awaken! Kaama, Krodha, Madha, Lobha, Moha and Matsarya are the six bandits who have burgled into your home. They are six enemies of the mind. These are the burglars who break into your fortress and rob your peace, good karma and well-being. *Kaama* is Lust, *Krodha* is anger, *Madha* is arrogance, *Lobha* is greed, *Moha* is delusion and *Matsarya* is jealousy. These negative forces will gradually drive away your goodness. Once your goodness goes away, you remain with only negativity and bad karma. Bad karma leads to bad consequences, which cause unhappiness and misery in this life and in after life if you believe in that.

If these vices are so well identified and clearly defined, why is it then a challenge to stay aloof from them? The problem is that these vices come to you in an attractive disguise. They allure your five senses and when they seductively hold your hand and walk along with you; it feels good for some time and you are on a new high. They rub themselves onto you and then you get embodied with the vices to display a vicious personality. The individual soul now gains a new identity as lustful, angry, arrogant, greedy, jealous and delusive fool. This overcoming of self by the vices is at such a profound level that it is very hard to shake off. Only a very drastic step under the strict guidance of a guru can help you out of the clutches of these vices.

The only right way is a safe precaution at the outset by not allowing these vices to capture you. A life of simplicity and walking down the straight path is easier said than done. The trouble begins with the words I, me or mine. The entire tussle in an ordinary human life is to bring as much into our own fold, i.e. how do I make this mine? This self-centrism does not permit inclusiveness; else instead of I, me and myself, we could give importance to US or WE. Once it becomes possible to include others, the collectivism becomes We.

Vasudhaiva Kutumbakam is the Indian philosophy, which means the entire world is one family. Agreed, it seems difficult to imagine such a blissful world, but that is the straight path. Waver a little this way or that way, but stay on course at least.

"A man who is of sound mind is one who keeps the inner madman under lock and key." - Paul Valery.

I have repurposed the brief description about the six inner vices from my Amazon #1 internationally bestselling book 'The Secrets to A Magical Life' just to set the context about what you can expect from this book.

What are negative emotions and vices?

Lust, Anger, Arrogance, Greed, Delusion and Jealousy are just commonly talked about six of the many vices. If the color white represents pristine positivity, and the color black represents a negative emotion, then there can be many shades of grey in between and we can give each a name, and define their characteristics based on the observation of the people and their behaviors. Likewise, we can extend the shades of these six vices, in as many as possible shades of grey.

Wiki says: Emotions are biological states associated with the nervous system brought on by neurophysiological changes variously associated with thoughts, feelings, behavioral responses, and pleasure or displeasure. Emotions produce different physiological, behavioral and cognitive changes.

Britannica says: Emotion is a complex experience of consciousness, sensation, and behavior reflecting the personal significance of a thing, event, or state of affairs.

The Merriam-Webster dictionary defines emotion as a conscious mental reaction (such as anger or fear) subjectively experienced as strong feeling usually directed toward a specific object and typically accompanied by physiological and behavioral changes in the body.

Going through various definitions for a word leads to interesting discovery. ***The crux of all definitions is that "emotion is the mental driver of physical actions."***

In my study about human emotions, I conclude it as: Emotions are the energy behind our actions. Energy is the driver, but the outcome can be different for different people under distinct circumstances. If the outcome is favorable, we call that positive and if unfavorable; we call it negative.

Anger is a vice, but to a certain extent, a mild form of it encourages you to stand up for a cause or against injustice and demand a resolute action. Greed is a vice, but the need to get something makes a person ambitious enough, and ambition gives rise to purposefulness. Jealousy is a vice, but a little dose of it enables competitiveness. Pride for honor is a strong positive emotion, but being too proud leads to arrogance. Fear is a vice, but to a small extent it invokes precaution against unnecessary danger. Passionate love requires the intensity of feelings, but unbridled obsession can become lust.

You get what you seek

His holiness Radhanath Swami said something interesting about human mindset. He said, we have much to learn from a honeybee. It travels from flower to flower and gathers nectar without harming them. It has a mindset that is focused on collecting the nectar even from a single isolated flower amidst miles of garbage around it. It teaches us the art of focusing on the positives and dealing appropriately with the faults. There will be faults everywhere and in every one, there is never a dearth of things to complain about. However, just as the honeybee seeks only the nectar we can aim to seek only the positive qualities in those around us.

Although each specie can be appreciated for its distinct nature, the fly represents a different mindset. Still we can learn relevant lessons from them to improve the quality of our own lives. On an otherwise healthy and clean body, the fly will focus only on sucking an infectious wound. A fly may travel across numerous flowers but it ignores the sweetest of fragrances and will focus on finding only on seeking garbage and excrement.

Develop a positive mindset to seek and appreciate only the good qualities in others. In doing so we also learn to focus on the good qualities in ourselves and overcome unhealthy low self-esteem.

The choice is yours whether to adopt the honey bee mentality or the fly mentality.

I appreciate your choice that by picking this book, you have chosen to spend some time in learning about awakening your inner conscience, and learn to deal with the negative forces of the mind, and overcome the pains in life that arises through them.

Awakened Conscience
Life is an excursion in stages and has conditions that helps us gain maturity. Life is

baffling, and best of all, a few of us can live a life of total engagement. As our ego and character become more grounded, the same techniques we used for endurance transform into hindrances. Life at that point offers a call to us, to awaken to our actual Self and permit ourselves to find our real essence. Individuals either seek psychological help outside, or there is an internal way, depending on oneself, to find the genuine Self. The breaking down of an individual's ego clears a path for change and the conceivable acknowledgment that completeness as a person is workable. The call to awaken can come at any stage, or age, in an individual's life. If we notice it, a higher condition of cognizance can arise and we can figure out the idea of the truth.

The soul is a power of the Divine Consciousness, which doesn't deteriorate, and aligns constantly towards Truth, Beauty and Bliss (Sat, Chit, Anand). In the eastern world, figuring out how to comprehend one's association with the heavenly is a piece of the instructive framework, though in the west, realism supplanted such a relationship, the nuclear family unit framework and an anti-religious rational attitude.

What to expect from this book?

This book delves into some of the vices more commonly faced by the people of this digital era. These vices are: Anger, Arrogance, Lust, Greed, Delusion, Confusion, Envy, Grief, Fear, Depression, Discrimination, Laziness, Loneliness, Hopelessness, Demotivation, Forgetfulness, Temptation, Sinfulness and Wandering mind. If anyone has never experienced any of these emotions at all, then it is probable that such a person has a fully awakened consciousness and would not require reading this book at all. However, if you have ever experienced any of these vices in your life and you seek answers on how to deal with them, then you are holding this key to solutions in your hand.

In providing solutions for dealing with these vices, you shall get introduced to the specific wisdom provided in the Bhagavad Gita. These solutions have been tested through time across 5000 years and the teachings of the Bhagavad Gita are still absolutely contemporary.

What is the Bhagavad Gita? Rajan Thapaliya says on Huff post: "Gita is one of the most influential treatise in eastern philosophy. The Bhagavad Gita is the eternal message of spiritual wisdom from ancient India. The word Gita means song, and the word Bhagavad means, God. Often we call the Bhagavad Gita the Song of God. It has shaped traditions and made eminent men for thousands of years. Spoken by Krishna to his disciple Arjuna at the battlefield of Kurukshetra, the Bhagavad Gita, answers major questions of our life and existence."

The teachings from the Bhagavad Gita have been corroborated with the conclusions from scientific research by scholars of behavioral science of the modern times and presented to the readers as absolute solutions that can never fail.

Also, this book emphasizes upon two strong wheels that drive the chariot our lives. They are (1) the art of forgiveness and (2) pursuing inner peace. These two virtues are essential elements for higher level of development in everyone's life.

Finally, this book guides you to the path of self-awakening through self-awareness. Self-awakening or spiritual awakening is the profound experience of dissolving the illusion that you are a separate entity from the oneness of this universe. In this, you use your energy to intelligently breakdown your obstacles, beginning with your ego. This process can get experienced through your body, senses, mind, and soul. Once you experience the inner flicker of light, you know you can use this illumination to clear up the darkness, illusion, pain, and misconception.

How to benefit from reading this book?

This book has original verses from the Bhagavad Gita in Sanskrit along with their English transcription and their translation as well. The gist of learning from the scriptures in the context of the topic is also provided. With these learnings as a base, solutions are provided in corroboration with modern theories of behavioural science. A spiritually awakened person is proficient in dealing with the inner vices and take charge of his/her own life. Hence, to begin with, let us inculcate some basic attributes of a self awakened person so that we can understand and appreciate each chapter and learn from them as we read. Later on, by the last chapter, you will understand in depth about attaining true self awakening.

The Bhagavad Gita has described the qualities of a self awakened person as follows:

श्रीभगवानुवाच:

अभयं सत्त्वसंशुद्धिर् ज्ञानयोगव्यवस्थिति: ।
दानं दमश्च यज्ञश्च स्वाध्यायस्तप आर्जवम् ॥

अहिंसा सत्यमक्रोधस्त्याग: शान्तिरपैशुनम् ।
दया भूतेष्वलोलुप्त्वंमार्दवं ह्रीरचापलम् ॥

तेज: क्षमा धृति: शौचमद्रोहो नातिमानिता ।
भवन्ति सम्पदं दैवीमभिजातस्य भारत ॥

sri-bhagavan-uvachah
abhyam sattva-samshuddhir
gyana-yoga-vyavasthitih

danam damashcha yagyashcha
swadhyayas-tapa arjavam

ahimsa satyam krodhas-tyagah
shatir-peshunam
daya bhuteshva-loluptam
mardavam hrira-achapalam

tejah kshama dhritih
shaucham-droho nati-manita
bhavati sampadam
daivim-abhijatasya bharata

The God said:
Fearlessness; purity of purpose; cultivating spiritual knowledge; charity; self-control; performing sacrifices; study of the Vedas; austerity; simplicity. -Sri Bhagavad Gita Ch.16; V.1.

Non-violence; truthfulness; freedom from anger; renunciation; tranquility; aversion to fault-finding; compassion for all living beings; non-covetousness; gentleness; modesty; steady determination. -Sri Bhagavad Gita Ch.16; V.2.

Vigour; forgiveness; fortitude; cleanliness; and freedom from envy and from the passion for honour, these transcendental qualities, O son of Bharata, belong to godly men endowed with divine nature. -Sri Bhagavad Gita Ch.16; V.3.

Attributes of a self-awakened person:

The scriptures have explained that a person with awakened consciousness is one who cultivates the following qualities in him/her and can deal with anger. Hence once should strive to gain such qualities.

1. **Fearlessness**–This is a wonderful trait to possess. It requires courage to initiate good things in life. It enables a person to channelize his/her passive anger into assertive anger to communicate the disagreement frankly and explore potential solutions.

2. **Purposefulness**–A person who is confident and purposeful in life is more likely not to succumb to negative emotions. Lack of purposefulness makes most people wander aimlessly in life, and such wanderers commit grave mistakes.

3. **Spirituality**–We are not human beings with spiritual experiences. We are spiritual beings with human experiences. A spiritual person is inclusive and humble about his own existence amidst the universe. Spirituality does not mean we have to reach the heaven, but it means that we must strive to make this place a heaven.

4. **Generosity**–A generous person who gives into charity and performs sacrifices understands we get what we give. He/she understands the power of sharing resources and helping others. Charity and kindness are not about giving away your surplus. It means, to share or give away something which you also need and could use.

5. **Simplicity**–A person who lives a life of simplicity and austerity shall often experience tranquillity and self-contentment. His/her behavior shall be modest and gentle. Such a person is highly unlikely to be stained by greed.

6. **Non-violence**–A person with awakened consciousness is non violent. He/she respects all beings in this creation and accepts differences.

7. **Truthfulness**–Truthfulness is the virtue which helps a person to stick to the path of

righteousness. A truthful person would not easily shift his/ her beliefs and facts for short-sighted benefits. When one doesn't lie to offend others, then one doesn't spread anger out of an anguish caused by lying.

8. **Aversion to fault-finding**–Finding fault with others originates from a superiority complex. Complexes whether of superiority or inferiority doesn't allow a person to be oneself. A conscious person realises humans make mistakes and nobody is absolutely perfect. One understands that pointing out faults will annoy others as much as cause anguish to self.

9. **Compassion**–Compassion towards all living beings elevates a person to the next level. Once you believe this universe is a singular source of energy and every being reflects the same energy, then there is no difference between one being and another. Every being is like a dew-drop that glistens like a pearl under the same sunlight. Such a person of awakened consciousness shall not try to hurt other beings.

10. **Determination and Vigour**–A person of awakened consciousness is full of steady determination and vigour. He/ she has a purposeful life and pursues life with positivity and self-confidence. Such persons are pursuing stronger emotions in their life and hardly succumb to anger.

11. **Non Covetousness**–A person with awakened consciousness doesn't covet what belongs to others. Covetousness is greed, and failure to feed the greed leads to dissatisfaction, and that leads to anger.

12. **Knowledge**–Gaining knowledge is a constant pursuit of a person with awakened consciousness. Gaining knowledge helps in understanding perspectives and provides wisdom to distinguish what is right and helps to make the right choices. In India there is a vast resource of

knowledge in Vedas, Puranas, Upanishads and other scriptures. To understand them, one has to study them from a holistic view and not just a religious view. This book is also an example of skimming specific knowledge from the Bhagavad Gita.

13. **Forgiveness**–Forgiveness is one of the greatest virtues of the humankind. Bearing a grudge is like a thorn imbedded in the flesh. Forgiveness doesn't mean approving the action of the wrong-doer, but it means that one has made a choice to move on ahead and leave the bad in the past. Such a person is forward looking and positive. Anger burns the inner self more than anyone else, whereas forgiveness helps with inner cleansing.

14. **Fortitude**–Fortitude comes in various forms like strength, courage and resilience. The weak and meek often succumb to anguish and anger compared to a courageous person who is much in control with his / her own life. They are the ones who can shape their own destiny without being flustered about actions and behaviours of others.

15. **Cleanliness**–Cleanliness of the body is what everyone understands, and cleanliness within is what everyone needs to learn. Our personality is all about accumulation of thoughts and memories generated from our experiences. We have to sort them and save the best parts while consciously remove the negative ones.

16. **Self-Control**–Freedom from vices comes majorly through self-control. Look into yourself whether you are easily excitable? Whether it can easily provoke you? Work on yourself to avoid getting manipulated at the hands of others and make your own wise choices.

17. **Freedom from envy**–Envy is an inferiority complex. A person who is an underachiever succumbs to the emotion of envy. The

universe gives what one deserves. Expand your capacities and make yourself more capable to receive.

18. **Renunciation**–Literally, this could mean to give away everything and desire for nothing. However, figuratively, it should read as the need to let go of excessive desires. Be practical, be wise. Keep your expectations more realistic.

"Once the soul awakens, the search begins and you can never go back. From then on, you are inflamed with a special longing that will never again let you linger in the lowlands of complacency and partial fulfilment. The eternal makes you urgent. You are loath to let compromise or the threat of danger hold you back from striving toward the summit of fulfilment." — John O'Donohue, *Anam Cara: A Book of Celtic Wisdom*

Chapter 1: CALMNESS FOR ANGER

What is anger?

Anger is an emotion characterized by antagonism towards someone or something you feel has deliberately done you wrong. It can give you a way to express negative feelings, or motivate you to find solutions to problems. Un-attended anger can cause harm to the physical and mental health of a person.

Sadhguru Jaggi Vasudev said, anger is not an entity somewhere that needs to be controlled or avoided. It is a situation created within us. The fundamental reason why anger is a problem is because our minds are not in our control, which needs to be addressed to. Situations must be created by human actions but right now situations are determining the human response.

Types of anger

Broadly, there are three types of expression of anger.
1. Passive Anger
2. Assertive Anger
3. Aggressive Anger

Passive Anger

One internalises passive anger, wherein the person avoids dealing with the situations and circumstances that contributed to the cause of anger. The victim may vent out his/her passive anger by withdrawing interaction with the wrong-doer, spread nasty rumours about him/her, damaging the belongings of such person, seeking opportunity to be mean to such person, holding a grudge and getting even when possible.

Assertive Anger

This expresses anger wherein the person communicates to the wrong-doer, his/her anguish over cause of anger in simple words like "I get angry when you ..." This is a good way to communicate the feelings of anger in a manner without threatening. It gives an opportunity to a person to mend ways and take corrective action to find a solution.

Aggressive Anger
This is an aggressive expression of anger wherein the person uses hurtful means to express his/her anguish by yelling, abusing, insulting, hitting, hurting or causing severe damages to the person or property of wrong-doer. This is an undesirable behaviour.

Wisdom from The Bhagavad Gita about anger

दुःखेष्वनुद्विग्नमनाः सुखेषु विगतस्पृहः ।
वीतरागभयक्रोधः स्थिधीर्मुनिरुच्यते ॥

duhkheshva-nudvigna-mahah
sukheshu vigata-sprihah
vit-raag-bhaya-krodhah
stidhir-muni-ruchhyate

One who is mentally undisturbed even amidst miseries, not elated when there is happiness, and who is free from attachment, fear, and anger, is a sage with a steady mind. -Sri Bhagavad Gita Ch.2; V.56.

क्रोधाद्भवति सम्मोहः सम्मोहात्स्मृतिविभ्रमः ।
स्मृतिभ्रंशाद् बुद्धिनाशो बुद्धिनाशात्प्रणश्यति ॥

krodhad-bhavati sammohah
sammohat-smriti-vibhramah
smriti-bhranshad-buddhi-nasho

buddhi-nashat-pranashyati

From anger arises delusion, and from delusion bewilderment of memory. When memory gets bewildered, intelligence gets destroyed and one falls down again into the trap of materialism. -Sri Bhagavad Gita Ch.2; V.63.

कामकरोधविमुक्तानां यतीनां यतचेतसाम् ।
अ भितो ब्रह्मनिर्वाणं वर्तते विदितात्मनाम् ॥

*kaam-krodh-vimuktanam
yatinam yata-cheta-saam
abhito brahma-nirvanam
vartate vidit-atmanam*

Those who are free from anger and all material desires, who are self realized, self-disciplined and constantly endeavoring for perfection, get assured of liberation by merging into the supreme being. -Sri Bhagavad Gita Ch.5; V.26.

Learning from the scriptures

We learned from the scriptures that a person can think in various ways according to his/her intelligence and mind-set. However, a person with a conscious mind is steady in his/her determination and uses the emotion of anger to express disagreement with a particular action. The aim of a conscious person is to arrive at a workable solution to the problem rather than create another counter-active problem.

Such a conscious person is unflustered amidst miseries and grounded amidst abundance of happiness. He/she stays detached from fear and anger.

People attached to material pursuits or objects of senses often succumb to desires and lust, which in the due course may become the cause of anger.

Anger causes delusion and bewilderment in the mind. Bewildered memory causes clouding over intelligence, because of which a person sinks into basic materialism.

Self-realised and self-disciplined persons make a constant endeavour for perfection and get liberated from anger caused by materialism and base desires.

Lust, anger and greed are the three pitfalls that lead to degradation of soul.

How to overcome anger?
We have understood what anger is and what are its various forms. We have also read from the ancient scriptures what wisdom it has shared through its teachings. The Bhagavad Gita has mentioned about superior human qualities and traits that one must possess. Now we shall analyse a few steps to understand how to overcome anger.

1. **Be Assertive**–As explained above, there are three types of anger: Passive, Assertive and Aggressive. While passive anger eats you from within, aggressive anger makes your behaviour anti-social. Adopt the path of assertion instead.

2. **Calm before you react**–Stay calm before you react. A well thought about action is always better than a spurt of violent reaction. Give yourself a few moments to gather your cool. Instead of a reaction, give a proper response.

3. **Express**–Do not hold a grudge. Speak up. Express your feelings and use your own point of view to express rather than using judgemental statement. For example, your child is playing all day and neglecting studies. Instead of yelling "You always neglect your studies..." try

saying as "It makes me upset if you neglect your studies and play all day." Now that's a constructive way to communicate.

4. **Offer Solutions**- While expressing your resentment, it is better to offer workable solutions. In the same example as above, while dealing with your child, if you say "I would be happier if you first finish your homework in the morning and then play for the rest of the day."

5. **Relax**–The heat generated inside you because of anger needs to be cooled down. Take refuge into humour and/or mediation regularly to keep your mind relaxed.

6. **Know when to seek help**–You should know when to seek professional help if you cannot manage your anger by yourself. Seek professional advice before it is late. A doctor can help with psychological counselling and psychiatric treatment using anti-depressant medicines. Never pop up over-the-counter medicines without professional advice.

Juna Mustad, a psychology counseller in her speech at TEDx Wabash College, said that anger is like a child that doesn't like to be stuffed in a trunk. Anger can be constructive or destructive. Most of us either stuff our anger or we suddenly find ourselves erupting in rage. She cited her own example that she tried to supress her anger in her toxic, abusive relationship just to avoid confrontation, and to the pleasure of her partner. Fight – Flight – Freeze are the common responses to anger. She went all around looking for solution and was running from herself until she paused, and turned around to face it. Here is what she advises to do when you are angry.

Clench your fist with your thumb within to relax the frontal cortex of your brain and breathe deeply to relax. Name your emotion, be kinder to yourself and inquire what action do I need to take right now. Anger hangs around until we take action to protest and confront it.

Senior psychiatrist Dr. Praveen Tripathi advises 3 steps to deal with anger.
1. Delay the reaction – By delaying your response, you shift your response from the reactive right brain to the logical left brain. The delayed response will be more logical and well thought of.
2. Anticipate the situation – Use your experience and wisdom to anticipate the situation and rehearse your response. See how best you can avoid a reactive situation.
3. Resolve the conflict – Usually there are repeated fights between two people about the same conflict. It is important that after a fight is over, both persons must discuss it in a calm situation to find a conslusive solution to resolve the conflict.

"Holding on to anger is like grasping a hot coal intending to throw it at someone else; you are the one who gets burned." – Buddha.

Chapter 2: MODESTY FOR ARROGANCE

What is arrogance?

Arrogance is "Madha'. It is the feeling in a person that he / she is better than rest of the people around, and is more capable of something one isn't. It is an overbearing sense of supremacy or self - importance. Apparently it seems over confidence but in fact it is under confidence which compels a person to become over-assertive about one's own superiority and try to gain greater control over every matter. Arrogance usually has a sharp tongue and a pointing finger.

If you ask an arrogant person whether he/she is aware of his/her arrogance, I'm sure you know that the answer would not be affirmative. However, you can clearly notice the arrogance in their behaviour. It will reflect as arriving late at work or in meetings, inturrupting others, bulldozing others' opinions and imposing self beliefs. Their self importance holds more weightage than the organisation. Their methods of work are mainly instructional and commanding rather than participative team-work. They despise the weak and have the urge to trample upon them instead of supporting and uplifting them. They can hardly accept an advice as constructive criticism. Anybody who confronts them are seen as enemies to be conquered. They have cruelty concealed below their false charm.

Types of arrogance
There are three types of arrogance.
1. Individual arrogance
2. Competitive arrogance
3. Antagonistic arrogance

Professor Nelson Cowan led a study with a team of psychology researchers at the University of Missouri-Columbia, and they broke them down into "levels."

1. **Individual arrogance.** This is most familiar. An over-sized estimation about one's own abilities or accomplishments which isn't. They resist any information that defines their limitations. They, are annoying, but harmless.

2. **Competitive arrogance.** Here person has an exaggerated sense of their own abilities or accomplishments as compared to others. They believe they can give the champions and stalwarts a run for their money. They have such a belief about their superiority that they fail to consider the perspective of others.

3. **Antagonistic arrogance.** This type is probably the most serious; the type of person who enjoys the denigration of others based on an assumption of superiority. Such an antagonistically arrogant person shows hostility towards others, displaying his / her aggression.

Wisdom from The Bhagavad Gita about arrogance

दम्भो दर्पोऽभिमानश्च क्रोध: पारुष्यमेव च ।
अज्ञानं चाभजितस्य पार्थ सम्पदमासुरीम् ॥

dambho darpo-abhimanash-cha
krodhah parushyamev cha
agyanam cha-abhi-jatasya
partha sampadam-asurim

Arrogance, pride, ego, anger, conceit, harshness and ignorance; O Partha, these qualities belong to those of a demoniac nature. -Sri Bhagavad Gita Ch.16; V.4.

इदमद्य मया लब्धमिमं प्राप्स्ये मनोरथम् ।
इदमस्तीदमपि मे भविष्यति पुनर्धनम् ॥
असौ मया हत: शत्रुर्हनिष्ये चापरानपि ।
ईश्वरोऽहमहं भोगी सिद्धोऽहं बलवान्सुखी ॥
आढ्योऽभिजनवानस्मि कोऽन्योऽस्ति सदृशो मया ।
यक्ष्ये दास्यामि मोदिष्य इत्यज्ञानविमोहिता: ॥

ida-madhya maya labdham-imam
praapasye manoratham
idam-astdam-api me
bhvishyati punar-dhanam

asau maya hatah
shatrur-nishye chaparan-api
ishwaroham aham bhogi
siddhoham balavaan-sukhi

adhyo-bhijanavan-asci
konyo-sti sadrishyo-maya
yakshye dasyami modishya
itya-gyan-vimohitah

The demoniac person thinks: I have so much wealth today, and I will gain more according to my plans. So much is mine now, and it will increase in the future. - Sri Bhagavad Gita Ch.16; V.13.

He was my enemy, and I have killed him, and I shall kill my other enemies too. I am the lord of everything. I am the benefactor. I am perfect, powerful and happy. I am the richest man, surrounded by aristocratic relatives. There is none so powerful and happy as I am. - Sri Bhagavad Gita Ch.16; V.14.

I shall perform some sacrifices, and give away some charity to absolve my sins, and thus I shall rejoice. In this way, ignorance deluded such persons. - Sri Bhagavad Gita Ch.16; V.15.

मुक्तसङ्गोऽनहंवाद धत्युत्साहसमन्वति: ।
सद्दिध्यसद्दिध्योर्नरिर्विकिर: कर्ता सात्त्वकि उच्यते ॥

mukta-sango-naham-vaadi
dhat-yutsaaha-samvintah
sidhya-ashidhyor-virvikarah
karta satvik uchhyate

One who performs his duty without being materialistic, without false ego, with great determination and enthusiasm, and without wavering in success or failure, performs with the intent of goodness. -Sri Bhagavad Gita Ch.18; V.26.

मच्चत्तित: सर्वदुर्गाणि मत्प्रसादात्तरष्यिसि।
अथ चेत्त्वमहङ्कारान्न श्रोष्यसि विनिङ्क्प्यसि॥

machhitah sarva-durgani
mat-prasadat-tarishyasi
atha chetatvam-ahankarann
shroyasi vinankashyasi

If you become conscious of Me, you will pass over all the obstacles of conditioned life by My grace. If, however, you do not work in such consciousness but act through false ego, not hearing Me, you will be lost. -Sri Bhagavad Gita Ch.18; V.58.

Learning from the scriptures

Pride, arrogance, conceit, anger, harshness and ignorance are the qualities of persons with negative attitude.

Arrogance manifests when a person assigns himself to extreme self-importance and thinks that he / she is the doer, the giver, and the central focus of everything. Pompous people who give to charity for the aim of self-proclamation are also arrogant people.

Un-confounded ego leads to delusion with ignorance. We desire a person should perform his/her duty without ego, with all enthusiasm and humility.

Nishkaam Karma is a term that means one performs his/her duty without expectation of anything in return for self.

One can overcome all obstacles in life by becoming conscious of HIM, the supreme universal energy. Submission with humility keeps the ego in check.

How to overcome arrogance?

That you can overcome arrogance expresses arrogance. The puffy feeling in the chest is unavoidable when you get showered with compliments. Humility is the only cure for arrogance. There are different ways to practice humility. Here are some examples.

1. **Submit to the supreme**–Whether you are religious or not, but you admit you are not the creator of everything and some other forces of energy is. Bow before the supreme forces above you. Keep your ego checked.

2. **Admit your mistake**–This sounds easy, but it is the hardest part to accept one's own fault and own it up. It is ego shattering and loss of face. It may embarrass oneself severely.

3. **Specific acts of humility**–Let us understand this with an example. The Sikh community of India are strong and boisterous people. They are hardworking and prosperous too. They volunteer services of humility at the Gurudwara, their place of worship. The 'sewadars' (volunteers) dust off shoes of the visitors, mop up

the floors, cook & serve food and wash the dishes too. Despite all their might, this method of community service makes them humble folks.

4. **Laugh at yourself**–We are humans and we all can goof up sometime. Laugh at your own folly. Be kind to yourself.

5. **It's okay to be imperfect**– Imperfect timely actions are better than inaction by waiting for perfection. Nobody is perfect in this world. Everyone is flawed to some extent. We can be more at peace with ourselves if we accept the imperfection in ourselves because once we do this, we can accept other people's imperfection as well.

6. **Allow others to take lead**–You don't have to be the boss everywhere in all committees, events or meetings. Allow others to take lead. Promulgate leadership and succession in your team. When your team grows in leadership, you get higher roles for yourself.

7. **Listen**–Be open to suggestions and new perspectives. Listen often and don't talk all the time. You can learn new perspectives only if you listen.

8. **Business before self**–Whether you are an entrepreneur or an employee, always put business before self. Learn to give yourself a lower priority than the organisation.

9. **Learn with humility**–When you learn something from someone, sit on the lower wrung. Knowledge is like water and it flows from above to beneath. Unless you sit with an empty glass, how can you receive any knowledge if you are already full. It means unlearn before you re-learn.

10. **Do not hesitate to seek help**– Admit it, you do not know everything and stop acting like 'know-it-all'. There are things you can learn from others, or seek help from people even below your ranks. Do not be shy to seek help. Your

knowledge will grow and your ego shall reduce. This is good for you on both counts.

11. **Practice gratitude**–Learn to say thank you to everyone who has done anything for you. People who express gratitude become humble and grounded. Grateful people attract more grace.

12. **Practice forgiveness**–Forgive yourself first and learn to forgive others as well. We must forgive others, because that is what we expect for our own mistakes.

13. **Seek honest feedback**–Learn to accept an honest criticism when you seek a feedback. If you expect people to say only good things about you, then it is better not to ask for any feedback. In a crowd of hundred admirers, you may also come across a few random trolls. Learn to take them in a stride.

14. **Male ego**–Unable to work under a female boss? Unable to let your wife or girlfriend drive the car or motorbike while you ride pillion? Can you let her take major decisions for the family? You can party out till late with your gang of guys. Can you let her party out late with her friends? Can you genuinely celebrate that your wife has advanced faster than you in her career and earns more than you? Check your inhibitions for these and many other such things. Let go of these inhibitions right away.

Dealing with arrogant people

Alexa Fischer is an LA-based actress and career coach, teaching others the skills to reach their goals in business and life. She has a theory that perhaps arrogant people are really insecure. Every time they display their arrogance, they try to tear you down a bit. How do you deal with difficulty, rudeness and arrogance? It might drive you crazy, but there is a way to have perspective and interface with arrogance so that everybody wins. Create a space. Do not react instantly. Take the suggestion, nod at it, mull over it. Later, use your confidence to convince the other person through encouragement mode and respond appropriately.

Self-confidence vs arrogance

Motivational speaker Gaur Gopal Das has put this into a brilliant perspective. Sometimes, there is so much humility that one keeps learning and never becomes good enough to compete. While some have acquired so much arrogance that they can't learn any more. He calls for the need to balance between humility and self-confidence so that your self-confidence doesn't go into the arena of arrogance. Self-confidence as he says, is not being better than others but being the best version of yourself. We have to compete with ourselves every time to become the best of our own ability. Now just because you have become the best version of yourself, doesn't mean that you have become the best in the world. The moment you claim that you are the best in the world, your self-confidence turns into arrogance.

We accept to learn from people higher than us and sometimes out of amusement from people lower than us. It is the hardest to learn from our equals. So self-confidence is about being open to learn from others around us. Dalai Lama said, when you speak, you only repeat what you already know, it is when you listen, you can learn more.

"If you aren't humble, whatever empathy you claim is false and probably results from some arrogance or the desire to control. But they root true empathy in humility and the understanding that there are many people with as much to contribute in life as you." -Anand Mahindra.

Chapter 3: REPUGNANCE TO LUST

What is lust?

Lust is 'kaama'. Lust is a psychological force producing an intense desire for an object, or circumstance while already having a significant other or amount of the desired object. Lust can take any form such as the lust for sexuality, love, money, or power. It can take such mundane forms as the lust for food (gluttony) as distinct from the need for food. It is like passion, but distinguished from it. Passion propels individuals to achieve benevolent goals whilst lust does not. [Wiki]

We majorly associated lust with sexual urges, having no foundation of love and respect. Such illicit desires instigate the person to commit immoral acts and hurt others while tarnishing themselves.

Types of lust
Lust can be of three types:
1. Lust in relationships
2. Lust for money/ wealth
3. Lust for power

Let us look into each of these forms of lust.
1. **Lust in relationships** – The person notices the body instead of the inner person. Wants just sex from his/her partner and not interested in talking or engaging in any activity together. Falls apart immediately after sex. Shuts off any communication if sex is denied.
2. **Lust for money** – No matter how much but it is never enough. There is a perpetual run for accumulating more, not for a purpose, but for insatiable lust for even more.

3. **Lust for power** – Another form of arrogance but lust for power is when there is no conscience, no morality.

Lust is not gender specific

Lust is not gender specific. It does not always flow from the male gender. It is a human vice and can be present among both genders. Here is an anecdote from The Ramayana depicting a lustful woman and her equally lustful brother.

Rama, Lakshmana, and Sita were dwelling in the forest after banishment from their kingdom. Shoorpnakha, the lustful sister of Ravana, eyed upon Rama. Rejected, dejected and insulted by both the brothers, she went to Ravana and apprised him about the beauty of Sita and incited him to kidnap her. The seeds of lust sown by the sister and harvested by the brother led to demolition of their entire clan and kingdom.

"Women have hunger two-fold, shyness four-fold, daring six fold, and lust eight-fold as compared to men."-Chanakya.

Wisdom from The Bhagavad Gita about lust

श्री भगवानुवाच

काम एष क्रोध एष रजोगुणसमुद्भवः ।

महाशनो महापाप्मा विद्ध्येनमिह वैरिणम् ॥

sri bhagavan uvacha
kaam esha krodha esha
rajo-guna-samudbhavah
mahaashano maha-paapma
viddhye-namiha vairinam

The God said: It is lust only, Arjuna, which is born of contact with the material mode of passion and later transformed into wrath, and which is the all-devouring sinful enemy of this world. -Sri Bhagavad Gita Ch.3; V.37.

तस्मात्त्वमिन्द्रियाण्यादौ नियम्य भरतर्षभ ।
पाप्मानं प्रजहि ह्येनं ज्ञानविज्ञाननाशनम् ॥

*tasmaat-tvam-indriyan-yadau
niyamya bharata-arshabha
paapmanam prajahi hyonam
gyan-vigyan-naashanam*

Therefore, O Arjuna, best of the Bharata clan, to begin with, curb this significant symbol of sin [lust] by regulating the senses, and slay this destroyer of knowledge and self-realization. -Sri Bhagavad Gita Ch.3; V.41.

एवं बुद्धेः परं बुद्ध्वा संस्तभ्यात्मानमात्मना ।
जहि शत्रुं महाबाहो कामरूपं दुरासदम् ॥

*evam buddhyeh param buddhva
sanstabhya-atmaanam-atmana
jahi shatrum maha-baaho
kaama-rupam durasadam*

Knowing oneself to be transcendental to the material senses, mind and intelligence, O mighty-armed Arjuna, one should steady the mind by deliberate spiritual intelligence and thus, by spiritual strength, conquer lust, this insatiable enemy. -Sri Bhagavad Gita Ch.3; V.43.

ये हि संस्पर्शजा भोगा दुःखयोनय एव ते ।
आद्यन्तवन्तः कौन्तेय न तेषु रमते बुधः ॥

*ye hi sam-sparsha-ja bhoga
duhkha-yonaya eva te
adhyanta-vantah kaunteya
na teshu ramate budhah*

The sources of misery are due to contact with the material senses. O son of Kunti, such pleasures have a beginning and an end, and so the wise man does not delight in them. -Sri Bhagavad Gita Ch.5; V.22.

ध्यायतो विषयान्पुंसः सङ्गस्तषूपजायते ।
सङ्गात्सञ्जायते कामः कामात्क्रोधोऽभजियते ॥

dhyayato vishayan-punsah
sangasta-shup-jayate
sangat-sajayate kamah
kamaat-krodho-bhijayate

While pursuing to gratify the senses, a person develops attachment for them. Lust develops from such attachment, and from lust, anger arises. -Sri Bhagavad Gita Ch.2; V.62.

Learning from the scriptures

Lust occurs from material desires, and unsatisfied lust turns into wrath. This becomes the cause for sinful actions.

Lust destroys our knowledge, discretion and self- realisation. Hence we must control our senses to prevent lust.

We should awaken our spiritual strength to make our mind steady through spiritual intelligence. Such a steady mind can conquer lust.

Wise people are cautious of the consequences, hence they do not indulge in material senses and hence do not succumb to lust.

Lust, anger and greed are the three gates to hell hence get rid of them to prevent degradation of the soul.

Since lust turns into wrath and later induces sinful actions, it is better to prevent lust at the outset.

How to prevent lust?

<u>Lust in a relationship</u>

1. **Love over lust**–Seek Love, Not Lust. There is a dividing line between love and lust. Love is to give in a relationship and lust is to crave

for receiving. You know you are succumbing to lust when you stop giving and start demanding in a relationship.

2. **Build relationship above the physical needs**–Can you have a healthy relationship without letting physical needs become the centre. Do you frequently abstain from lustful sex, and if so, for how long? Your relationship must have several elements to look for, besides physical needs alone.

3. **Mutual respect**–Respect each other's body and never take it for granted. 'No' doesn't imply 'Yes' in a relationship. Treat the partner as an individual and not as your property. Never force yourself upon each other. Know that the other person's body does not belong to you, so never intend to use or hurt them.

4. **Develop common activities together**–Do you come close in contact with each other only for sex? Develop other common and exciting activities between you. Develop a connection of friendly companionship. Try adventure sports, jogging, walking, long drive and such activities that pump up your adrenaline and enjoy it together as common interests. Even cooking together or watching a movie together are simple acts of love. When you have several things of common interest to do together, then physical attraction doesn't become the sole foundation of your relationship.

5. **Abstain from traps**–Do you indulge in watching porn? Do you often flirt casually? Perhaps you would say, "Huh! That doesn't fluster me." You never know that it incites unhealthy desires and your eyes get trained to see everyone as objects of carnal desires. Hence please abstain from consuming these graphics that pervert the mind.

6. **Nip in the bud** - Lust is a voluptuous emotion and it can gain toxic proportions. Nip it in the bud, otherwise it can become addictive. If something tempts you, look away. Block these attractions and distract your mind elsewhere.

7. **Avoid drugs and alcohol**–Avoid substances that numbs your mind and restricts your logical thinking. Often lustful crimes get committed by inebriated minds. Also, an inebriated mind is simple to manipulate by a miscreant.

8. **Improve your social manners**– When interacting with people and talking to them, look into their eyes and don't talk to their body parts. Do not touch them frequently, unnecessarily. Remember that handshakes should just be a professional handshake and not a crushing, lingering clenching of hand. Meet and interact at safe places, at socially acceptable timings and maintain respectable distance.

"Sex is the consolation you have when you can't have love." — Gabriel García Márquez

Lust for money

1. **Ambition vs Lust**–There is a difference between ambition to earn and lust for hoarding money. Observe yourself if you are greedy, miserly and cash hoarding personality like uncle Scoorge. Money by itself, doesn't give pleasure, but how you use the money does.

2. **Learn to use money**–Money is an enabler, and it is a safety net. You know you have the lust for money if you want to show off pompously rather than using effectively.

3. **Practice charity**–Practice charity. Decide a certain percentage. Say as little as 1%. Set aside this 1% out of every earning and give it to charity. Your donation will grow in absolute terms as your income grows. You will learn to be

comfortable to part with money without receiving something in return.

    4.   **Don't run after it**–Don't run after money but attract it towards you. Upskill yourself and make yourself eligible to receive the abundance in life.

    5.   **Don't resort to unlawful means**–Earn as much as your skill enables you, but do not resort to unlawful means to amass wealth.

"Money is like love; it kills slowly and painfully the one who withholds it, and enlivens the other who turns it on his fellow man."-Kahlil Gibran.

Lust for Power
    1.   **Lead, not dominate**–There is a dividing line between leading and dominating. To lead is to show the way to your team, but to dominate is to subjugate them to your command. Do not dominate.

    2.   **Share power** - Learn to collaborate and allow space for others also to contribute. Do not bulldoze the aspirations of people around you.

    3.   **Use lawful means**–Do not indulge in criminal activities to grab power. Stay within the legal framework. Accept that no matter how good you are, you will definitely meet with an opposition. Learn to co-exist and not vanquish them.

How Shiva overcame his lust?

Sadhguru Jaggi Vasudev told about lust as follows: Lust is a sense of incompleteness within you and a longing for something. The two eyes can see and perceive only that which is physical.

Shiva was meditating. The God of lust Kama Deva hid behind a tree, made an arrow of spring flowers and aimed it with a sugarcane bow, and delivered the bolt on Shiva's chest. It disturbed his meditative state. He saw Kama Deva right in front of him. He opened his third eye and fiery rays from it burnt Kama Deva into ashes which Shiva smeared on his body. Now this is a story told to the masses.

The third eye is an inward focussed eye looking within you. Your feelings of lust are not externally generated. It is an occurance within you. Essentially, Shiva might have experienced the incompleteness within himself and he with the help of his inward focuss, overcame his lust. The ashes on his body denote calm and peace after demolition of the fire within.

Why Budhha allowed a monk to stay with a prostitute?

The monks are supposed to wander, beg for alms and not stay in a household beyond two nights. There is an exception to the rule for the monsoon season when they can seek shelter and food in a household for two and a half months. One such monsoon, when Buddha and his followers were seeking shelters in a town, one of his followers Anandateertha was offered shelter by a prostitute. Ananda went to Budhha to ask for his permission. Budhha allowed, but others were disturbed. Budhha said "I have chosen this path of virtuous living. If her path is higher than mine, then as a seeker I must follow her too." Time went by, Ananda was offered silk robes, warm food, and the woman used to sing and dance before him. After two and a half months, Ananda returned with a female monk towing his trail. This is the power of virtuous living as narrated by Sadhguru.

"Chief among the forces affecting political folly is lust for power, named by Tacitus as the most flagrant of all the passions. Because power over others can only satisfy it, government is its

favorite field of exercise. Business offers a kind of power, but only to the very successful at the top, and without the dominion and titles and red carpets and motorcycle escorts of public office."- Barbara Tuchman.

Chapter 4: ALTRUISM OVER GREED

What is greed?

Greed is 'lobha'. Greed is an impulsive, excessively selfish desire for more of anything than needed. It is an uncontrolled longing for material gains. It has been undesirable throughout human history because it creates behaviour conflict between personal and social goals and also is a perpetrator of crime. A desire for progressive growth is ambition, but greed is the thirst to amass everything over actually required. Greed is a bottomless pit which exhausts the person with an endless effort to satisfy the need without ever reaching satisfaction.

A Greek scholar Socrates said: *"He who is not contented with what he has, would not be contented with what he would like to have."*

Types of greed
Greed can be of three types:
1. Greed due to lack of resources
2. Greed due to comparison
3. Greed due to want of hoarding

Let us examine the types of greed to put this into a perspective.
1. **Lack of resources** – There is an over-bearing desire to get everything when one doesn't have even the basic necessities. Lack of resources causes a gloat in the eyes out of sheer hunger.
2. **Comparison** – When one compares with others who have more, then out of sheer

comparison, greed arises to crave for more irrespective of one's own eligibility and ability.

3. **Desire for hoarding** – Looking at the accumulated treasure gives a feeling of high. Gradually, the person becomes a miser and aims at hoarding even more.

Wisdom from The Bhagavad Gita about greed

सत्त्वात्सञ्जायते ज्ञानं रजसो लोभ एव च ।
प्रमादमोहौ तमसो भवतोऽज्ञानमेव च ॥

satvatta-sanjayate gyanam
rajaso lobha eva cha
pamaad-mohau tamaso
bhavato-gyanam-eva cha

Actual knowledge develops from the mode of goodness; greed develops from the mode of passion; and from the mode of ignorance develop foolishness, madness and illusion. -Sri Bhagavad Gita Ch.14; V.17.

तदत्ियनभिसिन्धाय फलं यज्ञतप: क्रिया: ।
दानक्रियाश्च विविधा: क्रियन्ते मोक्षकाङ्क्षिभि: ॥

tadityan-abhi-sandhyaya
phalam yagya-tapah kriyah
dana-krishcha vividhah
kriyante moksha-kank-shibhih

One should perform various kinds of sacrifice, penance and charity without desiring fruitful results. The purpose of such transcendental activities is to get free from material entanglement. -Sri Bhagavad Gita Ch.17; V.25.

Learning from the scriptures

Actual knowledge comes from the path of goodness. Greed comes from excessive passion. From ignorance comes foolishness, madness and illusion.

Greed is one of the three gates to hell, besides lust and anger.

One should practice charity and sacrifice without any expectation in return. This helps people to part with their belongings systematically and also helps in the reduction of greed.

How to control greed?

1. **Patience**–Life is not a sprint but a marathon. Do not succumb to any get rich quick scheme. Learn the pace that things take time to bring reward.

2. **Inculcate generosity**–Learn to give and experience the pleasure in giving. Also, remember and appreciate people who have been generous to you.

3. **It won't go with you**–Remember when you came into this world, you brought nothing with you and nothing would go with you. Whatever you gain in this material world shall stay back right here for the others to use. Hence live a life of fulfilment and experience the joys of life while you can.

4. **It has no end**–You should know that greed has no end. It does not end after you accumulate a certain amount. Satisfaction of one greed gives rise to another. How long can you chase in a race that has no end?

5. **Control ego**–Greed comes because of ego. The feeling 'I deserve more' shall feed the greed. Be humble and be grateful. Practice gratitude for what you have got.

6. **Pleasure vs Peace**–Material things can give pleasure but not peace, satisfaction and happiness. Pleasures are short-lived.

The Science of Greed

Paul K. Piff is a social psychologist and research scientist in the Psychology Department at the University of California, Berkeley. In his talk at the TEDx Marin he described about a research he conducted with people playing a game of Monopoly and he observed their behaviour through a hidden camera. The guy who was winning most wealth during the game, was most pompous and excited. He also consumed most of the cookies kept at that table. He clearly displayed himself as the person wielding power. Paul observed that as a person gathers more wealth, his sense of entitlement and self-interest increases and his compassion and empathy towards others decreases.

In California it is a law for cars to stop for pedestrians crossing the road. In one such experiment, Paul observed that the drivers in a less expensive car were more likely to stop and abide by the law. As the expensiveness of the car increased, there were less chances of them abiding by the law.

In his talk on the Science of Greed, Paul said that amassing huge wealth may seem like an undisputable virtue but it has a significant cost attached. The ideology of self-interest could be the cause for social degradation. Something must be done about it before it is too late. So what should be done? He observed that even small changes and nudges about cooperation, community and compassion can help improve the egalitarian views. There has to be a constant effort towards bringing those small changes.

"Greed is the lack of confidence in one's own ability to create." -Vanna Bonta

Chapter 5: CLARITY OVER BEWILDERMENT

What is bewilderment?

Bewilderment is confusion. There is perplexity in every step. A bewildered person may find it hard to focus and may get worked up or upset for no reason. The major reason you feel confused and stuck is that you are afraid of making a mistake. You are afraid of failing.

In life there is no such thing called 'failure', because everything is just an experience. No one makes a poor decision knowingly. While deciding, everyone hopes it will deliver the desired outcome. However, the result of your decision may be favourable to you or otherwise. Hence, if the outcome is un-favourable, you may call it a poor decision on a hindsight. A delirious person is too scared of a negative outcome, hence delays or avoids any action.

One gets confused because one lives by one's own mind in the world of perceptions where no perception is the ultimate truth. We can never conclude the future based on the past. We can predict or estimate, but no prediction can ever define reality.

Life is always uncertain, the mind always seeks certainty and hence the conflict and confusion. There is no such thing as the right decision, it's just one direction that your life heads in. It could be destiny. All directions ultimately merge into the path of seeking knowledge. The mind in its ignorance believes in the concept of right decision.

Types of bewilderment

There can be three types of bewilderment.

1. Hypoactive
2. Hyperactive
3. Mixed

Let us understand the three types of bewilderment.

1. **Hypoactive** confusion leads to low activity. In this state of mind one acts sleepy or remains withdrawn or "out of it."

2. **Hyperactive** confusion leads to high-activity. In this state of mind, one acts upset, nervous, and agitated.

3. **Mixed** - A combination of hypoactive and hyperactive confusion.

Wisdom from The Bhagavad Gita about bewilderment

कार्पण्यदोषोपहतस्वभावः
पृच्छामि त्वां धर्मसम्मूढचेताः ।
यच्छ्रेयः स्यान्निश्चितं ब्रूहि तन्मे
शिष्यस्तेऽहं शाधि मां त्वां प्रपन्नम् ॥

karpanya-dosho-pahata-svabhaavah
prichhami tvam dharmasyam-moodha-chetah
yachhreyah syan-nishchitam broohi tanme
shishyasteham shaadhi mam tvam prapannam

Now I am confused about my duty and have lost all composure because of miserable weakness. In this condition, I am asking You to guide me for certain what is best for me. Now I am Your disciple, and a soul surrendered unto You. Please instruct me. -Sri Bhagavad Gita Ch.2; V.7.

व्यामिश्रेणेव वाक्येन बुद्धिं मोहयसीव मे ।
तदेकं वद निश्चित्य येन श्रेयोऽहमाप्नुयाम् ॥

vyami-shre-neva vakyena

buddhim moha-yaseeva me
tadekam vada nischatya
yena shreyoham-apunyam

Your equivocal instructions bewilder my intelligence. Therefore, please tell me decisively which will be most beneficial for me. -Sri Bhagavad Gita Ch.3; V.2.

ईश्वर: सर्वभूतानां हृद्देशेऽर्जुन तिष्ठति ।
भ्रामयन्सर्वभूतानि यन्त्रारूढानि मायया ॥

ishwarah sarva-bhutanam
hriddyeshe-arjuna tishtathi
bhramyan-sarva-bhutani
yantra-rudhaani maayaya

The Lord dwells in everyone's heart, O Arjuna, and is directing the wanderings of all living entities, who ride on a machine, made of the material energy. -Sri Bhagavad Gita Ch.18; V.61.

Learning from the scriptures

Despite his intelligence, Arjuna failed to figure out that his affection for his kin and his desire to protect them from death were the causes of his perplexity. Though he agreed that his duty was to fight in the battle, still on account of his inner weakness, he could not discharge the duties. He therefore asked Lord Krishna, the supreme spiritual master, to provide a definite solution.

Although Krishna did not intend to confuse Arjuna by any jugglery of words, Arjuna could not follow the process of Krishna consciousness, either by lethargic inertia or by active service. Hence he is inquisitive to clear the path of Krishna consciousness for all people who seriously want to understand the mystery.

After rebirth, the living entity forgets his/her past deeds, but the Super-soul, as the knower of the past, present and future, remains the witness of all his activities. Material nature fashions a particular type of body to a particular type of living entity so that he may work according to his past desires. We know this balance of karma from the past life as 'prarabdha' which becomes necessary to be fulfilled in this life.

How to avoid bewilderment?

1. **Seek a mentor** - The Vedic wisdom therefore advises that in order to solve the perplexities of life and to understand the science of the solution, one must approach a spiritual master who was under the guidance of a superior spiritual master.

2. **Justify being human** - One who doesn't solve his problems in life as a human leaves this world incognito like any other inferior animal. Humans pursue self–realisation and thus aim to solve their life's problems.

3. **Be optimistic**–Be optimistic about your own abilities, so believe in yourself that you can bring about a change.

4. **Do not generalise**–If you had a tough childhood, that should not get generalised as you will have a miserable future all your life. Such an attitude gets you nowhere.

5. **Do not blame yourself**–If you blame yourself for every mishap that happened everywhere, even if you were not there, then avoid being a paranoid.

"Understanding may become misunderstanding, if no commitment or no responsibilities are assumed, no specific objectives set, no definite expectations met, and common values and interests no longer shared. Mutual understanding may then, against all odds, end up in heartache, confusion and bewilderment." —Erik Pevernagie.

Chapter 6: CHEER OVER JEALOUSY

What is jealousy?

Jealousy is 'matsarya'. Jealousy or envy is a feeling of discontented or resentful longing aroused by someone else's possessions, qualities, or luck. Jealousy is a milder form of envy akin to desirousness, but envy is a dark side depicting intolerance for the abundance of another person.

Aristotle defined envy as pain at the sight of another's good fortune, stirred by those who have what we ought to have. Bertrand Russell said that envy was one of the most potent causes of unhappiness. Not only is the envious person rendered unhappy by their envy, Russell argued, but that person may also wish to inflict misfortune on others to reduce their status.

Envy can assume strange proportions. Sometimes, the feeling of envy comes from ignorance. It is a common psychological disorder seen in adolescent children when they are unacceptable of the physical relationship between their parents, or envy their siblings for the attention they get from their parents.

Types of jealousy
Jealousy can be of three types.
1. Rational jealousy
2. Irrational jealousy
3. Intentional jealousy

Let us analyse the three types of jealousy or envy.

1. **Rational jealousy**—In this type of jealousy, there could be a reason because of which one feels jealous of another. For example, in a relationship, if one partner is paying obvious attention and showing interest in a third person, then there is reason enough to be jealous. The feelings of romance and sexuality are very obsessive and exclusive. It could lead to OCD (Obsessive Compulsive Disorder).

2. **Irrational jealousy**—This is a kind of pathological jealousy in which one could feel an obsession even in the absence of any obvious reason. They could base the suspicion on imagination and fear of sharing or losing the loved one. Prolonged feelings could lead to depression.

3. **Intentional jealousy**—In this kind, one person intentionally acts or behaves in a manner to create jealousy in the mind or the other to entice a feeling or call for action. For example, if a person wants the partner to commit to a relationship, he/she acts in a flirting manner so that the partner he/she is interested in should feel jealous and immediately express commitment out of the fear of losing.

Wisdom from The Bhagavad Gita about jealousy

अद्वेष्टा सर्वभूतानां मैत्र: करुण एव च ।
निर्ममो निरहङ्कार: समदु:ख सुख: क्षमी ॥
सन्तुष्ट: सततं योगी यतात्मा दृढनिश्चय: ।
मय्यर्पितमनोबुद्धिर्यो मद्भक्त: स मे प्रिय: ॥

adveshta sarva-Bhutanam
maitrah karun eva cha
nirmamo nir-ahankarah
sama-duhkhah sukhah kshami

santushtah santata yogi
yatatma dridha-nishchaya
may-yarpit-mano-buddhiryo
mad-bhaktah sa me priyah

One who is not envious, instead, is a kind friend to all living beings; does not think himself a proprietor and is free from false ego; is equal in both happiness and distress, who is tolerant, always satisfied, self-controlled, and engaged in devotional service with determination, his mind and intelligence fixed on Me, such a devotee of Mine is very dear to Me. -Sri Bhagavad Gita Ch.12; V.13-14.

तानहं द्वषित: क्रूरान्संसारेषु नराधमान् ।
क्षिपाम्यजस्रमशुभानासुरीष्वेव योनिषु ॥

taanaham dvishatah
kruran-sansareshu naradhaman
kshipyam-ajsram-ashubhan
asurishvev yonishu

Those who are the lowest among people are envious and mischievous. I cast them into the ocean of material existence, and into various demoniac forms of life. -Sri Bhagavad Gita Ch.16 V.19.

श्रद्धावाननसूयश्च शृणुयादपि यो नर: ।
सोऽपि मुक्त: शुभाँल्लोकान्प्राप्नुयात्पुण्यकर्मणाम् ॥

sraddhavan-anasuyash-cha
shurnu-yadapi yo narah
soapi muktah shumbhamllokan
prapnu-yatpunya-karmanam

One who listens with faith and without envy becomes free from sinful reactions and attains salvation along with the pious people. -Sri Bhagavad Gita Ch.18; V.71.

Learning from the scriptures

Nothing ever flusters a person of awakened consciousness in any circumstances. Nor does he envy anyone. Such people take easily to consciousness.

An ignorant person may disagree to accept the existence of a supreme being, and he may act according to his own whims. However, his next birth will depend upon the discretion of the supreme. It is stated that an individual soul, after his/her death, gets placed into the womb of a mother where he gets a particular type of body under the supervision of superior power. Therefore, in the material existence we find so many species of life.

A righteous person can attain the planetary position of the pole-star. It is a metaphorical reference to a person assuming a nodal position and becomes a point of reference or an example to others.

How to avoid envy?
1. **Recognize envy**–To recognise and accept that you are envious of someone is the first step. The biggest challenge lies in accepting that you have a mental vice that you need to do something about. For any treatment, it is necessary to first diagnose the problem so that it can administer a remedy.

Chanakya once said: *"The learned are envied by the foolish; rich men by the poor; chaste women by adulteresses; and beautiful ladies by ugly ones."*

2. **Practice gratitude**–Count your blessings. Practice writing a daily journal of gratitude. Write things you are grateful for. To envy is to count the blessings of other people and then

regret it. The counter action is to count your own blessings. This will make you not only appreciate your own blessings but also help to build positive affirmations and attract positivity from the universe.

3. **Develop an abundance mindset**–A person who thinks and believes that he/she has abundance in life, often achieves more in life as compared to the one who always feels impoverished. This has to do something with the law of attraction.

Poet Tulsidas once said in his epic The Ramayana: 'All abundance is available in this world, but the unfortunate does not get.'

He further adds on: 'Nothing is unachievable for the capable one.'

Hence we learn that instead of envying someone for what they have, make yourself more capable and deserving.

4. **Remember that nobody has it all**–List out health, wealth, family, relationship, education, social recognition, and other pillars of your life. Now give scores to each pillar as +1 or zero or -1, being +1 for superb, zero for average, -1 for poor. If you sum up, an average person will find his/ her score near to zero. This experiment tells us that nobody has it all. Everyone gets abundance in one thing at the cost of another.

5. **Avoid comparisons**–Comparison begins from childhood. We hardly know what to expect in life until we see someone's success or possession and then desire to have similar. The other child scored higher grades than your child, the other guy earns more than you, the other person has a better spouse than yours and all these comparisons vex your mind. You compare the physical attributes one is born with; you compare all material belongings, and you even compare your

pet dog. Where is the limit to comparison? Stop comparing and accept yourself for what you are.

6. **Respect your own values**–You were born with some set of values and with time, you have gained some values that you are proud of. Respect your own values and culture. Be a unique original of yourself than being an inferior copy of another person.

The problem with most people is that they are more flustered with the growth and success of others than their own miseries. There is no sweeter sound than the sound of crumbling of a fellow person. Such is the demeanour of an envious person. Such a person keeps smouldering in his/her heart and burns one's own inner peace. Envy cannot help anyone achieve anything better. Instead, one should make continuous efforts to improve the self and make oneself more capable of receiving the best things in life.

A Monk's Approach

Ven. Nick Satajitto is a monk in a Thailand monastery. He shares these 5 tips to deal with jealousy.

1. **Do not compare with others** – If you compare with others, you will feel inadequate. See the good in others, make a list of them. Then use these qualities and try to integrate into yourself. He maintained a notebook and allocated two pages for each brother in the monastery. Whenever he observed a good quality in others, he used to write them down. Gradually he tried to integrate those qualities into himself.

2. **Anumotanaboon** – Rejoice your merits. Whenever someone did something good or commendable in the monastery, the others cheered for him as 'anumotanaboon!' When people do good, let's cheer them, encourage and rejoice good deeds.

3. **Spread loving kindness** – After meditation, in a calm state of mind, he could experience himself in a bubble of compassion around him. Being kind to oneself is the first step. Gradually expand this bubble as far as you can and shower your kindness on as many people.

4. **Talk to them and ask them how** – When he found another person more capable and efficient than him, then he approached him and asked how he developed those qualities that he admired. What techniques did he use? Can he share any tips so that someone can learn? Most people are willing to share the stories of their success if you inquire genuinely with an intent to learn. They might hand over their wisdom to you on a silver platter.

5. **Everyone experiences suffering** – Buddha discovered that the pains of birth, ageing, sickness and death are experienced by everyone. It is untrue to assume that others are not suffering. Even the rich and famous have to experience some suffering of their own and have to face challenges to deal with.

He sums up with the advice to keep cultivating your own serenity and peace to become your own refuge.

1. See yourself as you are
2. See others as they are
3. See your situation as it is

"Do not overrate what you have received, nor envy others. He who envies others does not get peace of mind."-Buddha.

Chapter 7: SOLACE AFTER GRIEF

What is grief?

Grief is 'moha' or intense attachment. Humans are social beings, hence the death of a beloved one causes grief. Grief is a strong and overwhelming emotion for people, regardless of whether their sadness stems from the loss of a loved one to which a bond or affection got formed, or from a terminal diagnosis they, or someone they love, have received. It is a normal process of reacting to a loss.

The loss may be physical (such as a death), social (such as divorce), or occupational (such as loss of job or money). You may experience all kinds of difficult and unexpected emotions, from shock or anger to disbelief, guilt, and profound sadness.

The pain of grief can also disrupt your physical health, making it difficult to sleep, eat, or even think straight. Although conventionally focused on the emotional response to loss, grief also has physical, cognitive, behavioral, social, cultural, spiritual, and philosophical dimensions. While the terms get often used interchangeably, bereavement refers to the state of loss, while grief is the reaction to that loss.

The grieving process

In 1969, psychiatrist Elisabeth Kubler-Ross introduced the 'five stages of grief.' These stages of grief got based on her studies of the feelings of patients facing terminal illness, but people have generalized them to other types of negative life changes and losses, such as the death of a loved one or a break-up.

The five stages of grief:
1. **Denial:** "This can't be happening to me."
2. **Anger:** "*Why* is this happening" Who is to blame?"
3. **Bargaining:** "Make this not happen, and in return I will ____."
4. **Depression:** "I'm too sad to do anything."
5. **Acceptance:** "I'm at peace with what happened."

If you are experiencing any of these emotions following a loss, it may help to know that your reaction is normal and you will heal soon. Everyone doesn't go through each of these stages. You do not have to go through each stage in order to heal. Some people resolve their grief without going through *any* of these stages. Also, if you go through these stages of grief, you probably won't experience them in a precise, sequential order, so don't worry about what you should feel or which stage you're supposed to be in.

Wisdom from The Bhagavad Gita about grief

देहिनोऽस्मिन्यथा देहे कौमारं यौवनं जरा ।
तथा देहान्तरप्राप्तिर्धीरस्तत्र न मुह्यति ॥

dehino-smin-yatha dehe
kaumaram yauvanam jara
tatha dehantar-praptir-

dhirastrat na muhyati

As the soul continuously transcends through this body, from childhood to youth and old age, the soul similarly passes into another body after death. Such a transition does not bewilder a wise person. –Sri Bhagavad Gita Ch.2; V.13.

न जायते म्रियते वा कदाचि-
न्नायं भूत्वा भविता वा न भूयः ।
अजो नित्यः शाश्वतोऽयं पुराणो
न हन्यते हन्यमाने शरीरे ॥

*na jayate mriyate va kata chinnayam
bhootva bhavita va na bhooyah
ajo nityah shashvatoyam purano
na hanyate hanya-mane shareere*

The soul is neither born nor dies and does not come into being. The soul is unborn, eternal, ever-existing and primeval and does not get slayed when the body gets slain. –Sri Bhagavad Gita Ch.2; V.20.

वासांसि जीर्णानि यथा विहाय
नवानि गृह्णाति नरोऽपराणि ।
तथा शरीराणि विहाय जीर्णा-
न्यन्यानि संयाति नवानि देही ॥

*vasaamsi jeernani yatha vihaya
navaani grihanati naro-parani
tatha sharirani vihay jeernani
anyani samyati navaani dehi*

As one gives up old clothes to put on the new, the soul similarly transcends from old and useless bodies to new. –Sri Bhagavad Gita Ch.2; V. 22.

अव्यक्तोऽयमचिन्त्योऽयमविकार्योऽयमुच्यते ।
तस्मादेवं विदित्वैनं नानुशोचितुमर्हसि ॥

*avyakto-yam-achintyo-yam
avikaryo-yam-uchhyate
tasmad-evam vidityenam
nanusho-chitum-arhasi*

The soul is invisible, inconceivable, and immutable. Knowing this, you should not grieve for the body. –Sri Bhagavad Gita Ch.2; V.25.

जातस्य हि ध्रुवो मृत्युर्ध्रुवं जन्म मृतस्य'च ।
तस्मादपर'ह'र्येऽर्थे न त्वं शोचितुमर्हसि ॥

*jatasya hi dhruvo mritur-dhruvam
janma mritasya-cha
tasmad-aprihar-yerthe
na tvam sochitum-arhasi*

One who is born shall die, and after death one shall be reborn again. Therefore, in the unavoidable discharge of your duty, you should not lament. –Sri Bhagavad Gita Ch.2; V. 27.

Learning from the scriptures

A delusional mind sees death as a painful end, but an enlightened mind knows that through death, the soul leaves one body and enters into another. Hence death is an act of rejuvenation to be rejoiced rather than grieved.

The soul is eternal, and it transcends from one body to another. It is immortal and indestructible.

One who lays down his life on the sacrificial altar, or in the proper battlefield, is at once cleansed of bodily reactions and promoted to a higher status of life. The process of re-birth is akin to changing from old clothes into new.

There is no source of knowing the identity of the father except by the authentication of the mother. Similarly, there is no source of understanding the soul except by studying the *Vedas*. The soul is inconceivable by human experimental knowledge. The soul is consciousness and conscious, that also is the statement of the *Vedas*, and we accept that. They oft repeated this concept in the *Vedas* and scriptures because repetition ensures thorough learning.

How to overcome grief?

1. **Healing**–It is a complex process. It is an emotional process, from distress and despair to recovery. There can be no one standard way of doing this because people are unique in their perceptions and different people react to situations differently. The process begins with accepting the absence of the loved one and then gradually reverting to the normal life.

2. **Time**–Each person needs a different span of time to pass through the grieving process. It all depends on the individuals. Some feel better in a few days, while some may take years.

3. **Cry**–Instead of putting up a brave face, standing tall, strong, and resilient, just cry. Cry even if you are a man and defy the cliché that men don't cry. It will only make you feel lighter.

4. **Socialise**–Go out and mingle with other people. Take part in social gatherings and celebrate the happiness of others. That would rub in some positivity on you as well.

5. **Embrace life**–Come to acceptance of the loss and try to move on. Moving on does not mean that you forget your loved one. Instead of saying "It's okay, my husband died," you may say "My husband died, but I shall be okay." You must

continue with your routine of eat, sleep and pray. Get back to your work at the soonest possible.

Swami Muktananda said, when you lose someone you loved, it is natural to experience a process. Expect these things to happen.

Disbelief – no it has not happened. I cannot believe it happened.

Denial – you deny that the person has not gone but is still around.

Guilt – did I fail in doing enough to save him?

Anger – against God for being unfair.

Then there is a period of grieving.

Once you have been through this process, you are expected to revert to normal life. Bring knowledge to yourself. We do not grieve when the Sun sets. Everything is temporary in this world. Seek the eternal relative, your soul's beloved, your God.

There's no such thing as moving on

Stand up comedian, actor, writer, Kelley Lynn in her talk at TEDx Adelphi University said that the phrases like 'you need to move on' or 'get over it' are phrases born out of centuries across centuries. Is it fair to take away the memories of people you loved? Are they replaceable? This is not the way to honour those whom we loved. Instead, 'Move with – Move through.' Great things happen when we continue to tell stories about people we love. Love grows more love. We all are going to die some day and we have no choice about that, but we have a choice about how we talk about the people we loved.

"You will lose someone you can't live without, and your heart will be badly broken, and the bad news is that you never completely get over the loss of your beloved. But this is also the good

news. They live forever in your broken heart that doesn't seal back up. And you come through. It's like having a broken leg that never heals perfectly—that still hurts when the weather gets cold, but you learn to dance with the limp."
— Anne Lamott.

Chapter 8: FORTITUDE AGAINST FEAR

What is fear?

Fear is the basic emotion of insecurity towards existential crisis. A lion is chasing a deer to make a kill. Fear drives both. The deer of course has fear of death, while the lion has the fear of hunger pangs and consequential death.

Fear is a natural, powerful, and primitive human emotion. It involves a universal biochemical response and a high individual emotional response. Fear comprises two primary reactions to some type of perceived threat: biochemical and emotional. Fear alerts us to danger or the threat of harm, whether that danger is physical or psychological.

Sometimes fear stems from genuine threats, but it can also originate from perceived dangers. Fear can also be a symptom of some mental health conditions including panic disorder, social anxiety disorder, phobias, and post traumatic stress disorder (PTSD).

The most common phobias experienced by humans are:
- Acrophobia-fear of heights.
- Aerophobia- fear of flying.
- Arachnophobia-fear of spiders.
- Astraphobia-fear of thunder and lightning.
- Autophobia-fear of being alone.
- Claustrophobia-fear of confined spaces.
- Homophobia-fear of blood.
- Hydrophobia-fear of water.

Types of fear
Fear can be of three types.

1. Primal
2. Rational
3. Irrational

Let us understand each of these three types of fear.

1. **Primal fear** – These are innate fears programmed into our brains. Some of these could be from birth. For example, fear from predators and snakes. Some fears can get programmed by experience or observation. For example, fear from fire or electric shock.

2. **Rational fear** – This occurs when there is a real, rational or imminent threat. For example, someone threatens you with a weapon. There is a real fear irrespective of the fact whether or not that person would actually attack you. Also, while walking through a crowded place, you are likely to clutch your bag firmly or hold your baby securely in your arms out of fear of losing them in the crowd.

3. **Irrational fear** – This kind of fear is perceived by individuals, and differ from person to person. There is no logical reason to justify it. For example, one could fear ghosts or even a face of a clown. A part of the brain fears it but the other part of the brain wonders why.

It is unwise to seek recluse because of fear. One has to go out of the comfort zone to confront and conquer the fear. As Dale Carnegie said: *"Inaction breeds doubt and fear. Action breeds confidence and courage. If you want to conquer fear, do not sit home and think about it. Go out and get busy."*

Wisdom from The Bhagavad Gita about fear

वीतरागभयक्रोधा मन्मया मामुपाश्रिताः ।
बहवो ज्ञानतपसा पूता मद्भावमागताः ॥

vita-raag-bhaya-krodha
man-maya mam-upashritah
bahavo gyan-tapasa
poota mad-bhavam agataah

Being freed from attachment, fear and anger, being fully absorbed in Me and taking refuge in Me, many people in the past became purified by awareness of Me, and thus they all attained transcendental love for Me. -Sri Bhagavad Gita Ch.4; V.10.

सञ्जय उवाच
इत्यर्जुनं वासुदेवस्तथोक्त्वा
स्वकं रूपं दर्शयामास भूयः ।
आश्वासयामास च भीतमेनं
भूत्वा पुनः सौम्यवपुर्महात्मा ॥

sanjaya uvacha
itya-arjunam vasudevas-tathoktva
svakam rupam darshayamas bhooyah
aashwayamas cha bhhetmenam
bhootva punah saumya-vapur-mahatma

Sanjaya said to Dhritarashtra: Lord Krishna, having spoken thus to Arjuna, displayed His real four-armed form and reverted to His two-armed form, thus encouraging the fearful Arjuna. –Sri Bhagavad Gita Ch.11; V.50.

प्रवृत्तिं च निवृत्तिं च कार्याकार्ये भयाभये ।
बन्धं मोक्षं च या वेत्ति बुद्धिः सा पार्थ सात्त्विकी ॥

pravrittim cha nivrittim cha
karya-akarye bhaya-bhaye

> bandhanam moksham cha ya vetti
> buddhih sa parth sattviki

O son of Pritha, the discretion of what ought to be done and what ought not to be done, what is to be feared and what is not to be, what is binding and what is liberating, is in the sattvik person. –Sri Bhagavad Gita Ch.18; V. 30.

Learning from the scriptures

People who get attached to the bodily conception of life are so absorbed in materialism that it is almost impossible for them to understand the existence of the Supreme. Such materialists cannot even imagine that there is a transcendental soul which is imperishable, full of knowledge and eternally blissful.

At the outset, one must have a preliminary desire for self-realization. This will bring one to the stage of trying to associate with persons who are spiritually elevated.

In the next stage one becomes started by an elevated spiritual master, and under his instruction the neophyte devotee begins the process of devotional service. By execution of devotional service under the guidance of the spiritual master, one becomes free from all material attachment, attains steadiness in self-realization, and gains a taste for learning about the Supreme.

The eyes have to be willing and receptive to see the eternal supreme as HE is.

One has to develop the discretion to know what action should get performed or not. Such justified action only can lead to liberation.

How to overcome fear?

1. **Know the Cause**–Get to know what causes your fear and anxiety. You can tackle a problem better when you understand it completely. What is the intensity of the threat? What are the stakes to lose? What are the various consequences and how they can get mitigated?

2. **Visualize success**–Visualise how a smart person in your place under similar circumstances would tackle it. What would be his/her decision-making strategy? Make note of the steps taken and probable outcomes. Fear is first conquered in the mind and then on the ground.

3. **Confront fear** - The best remedy to handle fear is to face it. The more you run away from it, the more it chases you down so turn back confront it. You can conquer something only if you confront it.

4. **Prepare for the worst**–Always know the maximum wavelength of the consequences. If you speak out righteously, what will be the worst likely outcome? Know the worst consequence and if it comes to that, how will you tackle that situation. This analysis helps you to eliminate unknown fear and makes you prepared to face the consequences of your action (or inaction).

5. **Consistent imperfect action**–Do not wait for a perfect plan. Take consistent imperfect actions. This will help you keep moving and gaining ground. For example, you fear that the project is complicated and may not progress smoothly. If you keep on working out a plan of perfection, you would lose more time and become delusional at a point in time. Instead, consistent imperfect action will let you progress until you gain confidence about finishing it.

6. **Lateral Thinking**–You cannot find alternative solutions if you stare harder and longer at the same thing. Think differently. View the problem from a different angle and a new

perspective. This will help generate newer and better solutions.

7. **Composure**–Maintain calm and composure when tackling a situation. We cannot draw proper solutions in a state of nervousness and anxiety. A calm and composed mind can think radically without bias and offer a workable solution.

8. **Medical help**–Seek medical help for morbid fears and phobias. A combination of medicines with counselling can help to win over this situation. However, the sooner you seek help, the better are the chances of success.

Your experiences shape your perceptions

His holiness Radhanath Swami narrated an interesting story to describe how our experiences shape our perceptions. Once he was meditating in the forests of Boudhanath valley in Nepal, he heard heavy footsteps. A well built European was walking down, carrying a grocery bag containing fruits. Soon a troop of gibberish monkeys surrounded him and were screeching. For a while, the man tried to shoo them off but as the monkeys advanced towards him, he was terrified. He threw the bag away. One of the monkeys grabbed it and ran away and others followed it. The man escaped in another direction.

Soon a local boy came running, wielding a stick in his hand. Looking at him, the monkeys got terrified and scattered away leaving the bag behind, taking shelter amongst the trees. The boy sat right there and ate the fruits right in front of the monkeys as they watched him silently.

What is the lesson learnt? The European had no prior experience with monkeys so when he met this situation, he was scared of the unknown. The boy who was just the size of one arm of that man, had enough experience with the monkeys so he knew how to handle them. The monkeys had no experience with the European so they did not know he could harm them but, they had enough prior experience with the boy and they knew he would beat them with a stick so they were fearful of the boy.

"I have learned over the years that when one's mind is made up; this diminishes fear; knowing what must be done does away with fear."-Rosa Parks.

Chapter 9: BLISS AFTER DEPRESSION

What is depression?

Depression, or major depressive disorder, is a common and serious yet treatable medical illness that negatively affects how you feel, the way you think and how you act. Depression causes feelings of sadness and/or a loss of interest in activities you once enjoyed. It can lead to a variety of emotional and physical problems and can decrease your ability to function at work and at home.

An enlarged and hyperactive amygdala (an almond-shaped grey matter in the brain that enables experience of emotions), along with abnormal activity in other parts of the brain, can cause disturbances in sleep and activity patterns. It can also cause the body to release irregular amounts of hormones and other chemicals in the body, leading to further complications.

Types of depression

There are eight different types of depression:

Clinical Depression - Clinical depression or major depression is when a doctor has given you a diagnosis of depression. They call it Major Depressive Disorder because one feels depressed most of the time for most of the days.

Persistent Depressive Disorder - If the depression lasts for 2 years or longer, it's called Persistent Depressive Disorder. This term is used to describe two conditions previously known as dysthymia (low-grade persistent depression) and chronic major depression.

Bipolar Disorder—Also called manic depression. It causes extreme mood swings between feeling elated and wretched.

Seasonal Affective Disorder (SAD)—It happens usually during winter season when sunlight it scarce. It can also occur every day immediately after sunset.

Psychotic Depression - The feeling of depression includes hallucinations (seeing or hearing things that do not exist), delusions (false beliefs), paranoia (wrongly believing that others are trying to cause a harm)

Situational Depression – Certain stressful situations could trigger the depression and can stay until the cause of stress remains.

Peripartum (Postpartum) Depression – Some women feel acute depression before or after childbirth.

Premenstrual Dysphoric Disorder (PMDD)—Symptoms include mood swings, anxiety, irritability, fatigue, and an overwhelming feeling.

Research suggests that continuing difficulties, long-term unemployment, living in an abusive or uncaring relationship, long-term isolation or loneliness, prolonged work stress, are more likely to cause depression than recent life stresses. Women are nearly twice as likely as men to be diagnosed with depression. Depression can occur at any age.

Here is a poem by Rupi Kaur that depicts the sentiments of a depressed person. For a normal and cheerful person, a morning would seem like a perfect meditative state of solitude with the Sun sitting on the horizon, flowers scattered all over the grass beds. She described a different imagery in this poem.

Depression is a shadow living inside me– Rupi Kaur

Yesterday
When I woke up,
The Sun fell to the ground and rolled away
Flowers beheaded themselves
All that is left alive here is me
And I barely feel like living

Wisdom from The Bhagavad Gita about depression

क्लैब्यं मा स्म गमः पार्थ नैतत्त्वय्युपपद्यते ।
क्षुद्ररं हृदयदौर्ब्यं त्यक्त्वोत्तिष्ठ परन्तप ॥

klaibyam maa sma gamah partha
naitat-tvay-upa-padhyate
kshudram-hridaya-daurbalyam
tyakta-vottishtha paran-tapa

O son of Pritha, do not yield to this degrading impotence. It does not become you. Give up such petty weakness of heart and arise, O chastiser of the enemy. –Sri Bhagavad Gita Ch.2; V.3.

मात्रास्पर्शास्तु कौन्तेय शीतोष्णसुखदुःखदाः ।
आगमापायिनोऽनित्यास्तांस्तितिक्षस्व भारत ॥

maatra-sparshastu kaunteya
shitoshna-sukha-dukhadah
aagama-payino-nityastam
stitikshrava-bharata

O son of Kunti, the temporary appearance of happiness and distress, and their disappearance in due course, are like the change of seasons. They arise from sense perception, O scion of Bharata, and one must learn to tolerate them without being disturbed. –Sri Bhagavad Gita Ch.2; V.14.

वेदाविनाशिनं नित्यं य एनमजमव्ययम् ।
कथं स पुरुषः पार्थ कं घातयति हन्ति किम् ॥

veda-vinashinam nityam
ya enam-ajam-avyayam
katham sa purushah partha
kam ghatayati hanti kam

O Partha, how can a person who knows that the soul is indestructible, eternal, unborn, and immutable kill anyone or cause anyone to kill? –Sri Bhagavad Gita Ch.2; V. 21.

Learning from the scriptures

Petty weakness of the mind leads to inaction and delusion. Not performing one's duty brings infamy. Do not succumb to depression to become unworthy of your birth because there are some spaces only you can fill in this world. In the proper discharge of duty, one has to learn to tolerate impermanent appearances and disappearances of happiness and distress. We base these experiences on sensory perceptions.

Overwhelmed with the consequences of action and over-personalisation for distant occurrences like "I hold myself responsible for this mishap, I wish I were there..." can overburden the mind.

How to treat depression?

Anxiety is a state of mind that can get gradually corrected with counselling, training and pacifying with medicines. Anyone can feel the blues and it gradually gets blown over. However, depression is an advanced stage of disorder which might require medical intervention.

Like other people, I too went through some rough patches in life. I could manage to sail through some difficult episodes with the strength of my inner-self through my learning in life, however, one episode was more severe when I needed medical help. My allopath gave me a long prescription of anti-depressants and sleep medicines. It looked scary, and I was sceptical about their long-term side effects. Also, talking with people who took similar treatment revealed that they were under such treatment for a considerable duration of time. So I went for homoeopathy. It worked for me. After six to eight months of medication and my simultaneous working on my inner-self, pulled me out of the situation completely.

A mild depression caused by certain occurrence of event can get over with changed circumstances. For example, depression caused by job loss, fallout in relationship, loss in business, or poor health, can be corrected when the circumstances revert to normal, like you get another job, you get another partner, your business grows well, you are healthy again. Time heals better than anything else.

During the phase of depression, one may feel like lying down, coiled up, in recluse, but this is the time to muster up your inner strength and prepare your body and mind for bearing the struggle. Things that you must compulsorily do during a phase of depression are:

1. **Sleep cycle**–You have to get sufficient sleep, even if with the help of some prescribed medicines. The mind gets most of its calming and rest during sleep. There is no benchmark for how much sleep is necessary. If you wake up without an alarm clock and without someone nudging you, and if you feel fresh after waking up, then you have slept enough.

2. **Meditation**–Meditation helps in strengthening your mind and your inner conscience. In my book The Secrets to a Magical Life, I have described various kinds of meditation and explained how to do it. You can get a copy for yourself to learn about meditation and many other useful hacks in life. However, for the benefit of my readers of this book, let me bring some excerpts here as well.

We can meditate in several ways.

Mindful Meditation -One way is mindful meditation, which we can do anywhere, anytime. Sit in a quiet and comfortable place in a calm posture, close your eyes, and focus your attention inward to a fixed point between your eyes. You are mindful of the world around you, but without reacting. You focus on your breathing, as I have explained earlier. Use this relaxation technique.

Transcendental Meditation -Another method is transcendental meditation, wherein you play some favourite mantra or natural sounds or music tunes to focus and concentrate with lesser effort than a mindful meditation and follow the same process as that thereafter.

Guided Meditation - Guided meditation is under the care and guidance of a guru or teacher who speaks in a manner to give you an imagery to focus upon. This is similar to Neuro Linguistic Programming, as discussed earlier.

Meditation Through Yoga - There is also meditation, along with certain postures of yoga that require greater balance. Maintaining the balance of postures helps to focus and concentrate better with brief distraction. It requires more practiced effort for the Chakra meditation or awakening the *Kundali*. It is a calm posture like the mindful meditation but for best results; do it preferably in the early morning hours after complete fasting through the night. It is a reverberation method wherein you focus on the path of your spine beginning from the anus and travel up step by step through belly, chest, throat, forehead and the top of the head. Chanting AUM in a base tone helps to reverberate and awaken the chakras hidden in your organs. It will require a lot of practice and the day you touch upon the fontanel you will experience bliss. The art of meditation is over-rated as an exclusive expertise, but it is much simpler.

Meditation must be a part of our daily routine. Though any time of the day when it is possible, would be fine if that works for you but early hours of the morning are the best ones. Meditation helps to reduce stress. It helps to control anxiety and promotes emotional health. It helps to enhance self-awareness and also helps to expand your attention span. Meditation also helps in improving memory and stops the degeneration of brain cells because of ageing. It is a major enabler for mental, emotional and spiritual well-being. Ramana Maharishi said, "*When there are thoughts, it is distraction: when there are no thoughts, it is meditation."*

3. **Exercise**–A moderate exercise is very important to beat depression. The body has to break free from the clutches of lethargy. Exercise under the open sky works best. Try to go into a park, or do it in your sit out, or your terrace. Get yourself a yoga mat to begin with a small routine. Exercise is not only about yoga. Walking, running, cycling, swimming, or any other sport helps as much.

4. **Breathing**–Controlled and mindful breathing helps in reducing stress. Once again, in my book The Secrets to A Magical Life, I have explained about the right breathing pattern that helps. Inhale deeply to fill your lungs and gradually release the breath with your lips puckered in the shape of O.

5. **Diet**–Eat nutritious, healthy fresh food. Do not eat processed food or industrially manufactured products. The best food is that which comes from plants. They are rich in proteins, minerals, vitamins and anti-oxidants. There are tough terrains on earth where vegetation is less. In that case, food can get sourced from animals as well.

6. **Reasoning**–The above five steps are to handle the well-being of your body. Besides those, engage yourself in mindful reasoning. Look at your situation from a distant view. Analyse the causes and list out potential solutions. Analyse the effect of those solutions to see what works best for you.

The Chemical Factory of Wellness

The body produces four hormones which are essential for our well being. Let us learn about what each of them does to us and how we can help produce them.

DOPAMINE—The reward hormone

Dopamine gets released when you complete a task and feel rewarded. It also gets produced when we take care of our body. Celebrating small wins and success, enjoying wonderful food or music, also helps trigger dopamine.

SEROTONIN—The mood stabiliser

It is a hormone that stabilises the mood and gets triggered with the help of physical and mental exercise. Meditation, yoga, walking, running, cycling, swimming, or any other form of outdoor sports help trigger serotonin.

ENDORPHIN—The pain killer

Laughter is the best medicine. Watch a comedy or do something funny. Fun activities, eating dark chocolates, and using aromatic essential oils also help to trigger endorphin.

OXYTOCIN—The love hormone

Love and compassion like holding hands, hugging, cuddling, caressing or love-making are sure triggers for oxytocin. It has same effects even when you play with or hug children and pets. It should trigger the feeling of love. It is important to love or to be loved. Even exchanging lovely compliments does the trick.

Our own body is the chemical factory of wellness, and now we know how to trigger these.

Support the mind

A mild fever in the body can arouse concern over the health. People over-rate physical illness but cannot recognise a mental agony. Do not be harsh to shun it off by calling it madness. Observe the trigger points and then do something about it. Merely living with those triggers may worsen the situation further. When the signs of depression are acute, i.e. you cannot sleep, eat or work normally, then do not hesitate to seek professional help. You can try to handle it all by yourself, but that would take longer and results may be elusive.

How Dwayne 'The Rock' Johnson fought depression

He was playing for the Calgary Stampeders in CFL and wanted to get into NFL but his coach cut him off. His dad Rocky Johnson was a wrestler in the 60s and 70s. He came to pick him up in his truck. Dwaye had just seven bucks with him. He was moving back to his parents' house. His life and dreams were shattered at the age of 23. He was depressed. For a month and a half, he found solace in just one thing, cleaning his apartment.

One fine day the coach called up and offered to take him back but he had moved on. He decided to be into the wrestling business. His father felt he was making a wrong choice but he said 'dad either you train me, or do not train me'. His father rose to the occasion and supported him. Dwayne realised that his assets were only his hands and body so he had to work with them. His father started training him.

He always keeps his back against the wall so that there is only one way to go and that's forward. Thereafter his life never looked back. He was into wrestling, entertainment, movies and other things.

Never forget where you came from and put that in front of you. Always hold your back against the wall, says Dwayne, hold on to the fundamental quality of faith, because on the other side of the pain, there is something good.

"It's so difficult to describe depression to someone who's never been there, because it's not sadness. I know sadness. Sadness is to cry and to feel. But it's that cold absence of feeling—that really hollowed-out feeling."- J. K. Rowling.

Chapter 10: EQUALITY OVER DISCRIMINATION

What is discrimination?

Discrimination is the act of making unjustified distinctions between human beings based on race, caste, gender, age, education, religion or any other categories.

The Indian philosophy further believes that every living being has the same reflection of the Supreme and the soul is transcendental between various life forms. Hence it is forbidden to hurt even an animal.

It is said that the total count of living beings remains the same. As the human species grew in numbers, the other animals got reduced by the same number.

According to Amnesty International, "At the heart of all forms of discrimination is prejudice based on concepts of identity, and the need to identify with a certain group. This can lead to division, hatred, and even the dehumanization of other people because they have a unique identity. In many parts of the world, the politics of blame and fear are on the rise. Intolerance, hatred and discrimination are causing an ever-widening rift in societies. The politics of fear is driving people apart as leaders peddle toxic rhetoric, blaming certain groups of people for social or economic problems."

Wisdom from The Bhagavad Gita about discrimination

विद्याविनयसम्पन्ने ब्राह्मणे गवि हस्तिनि ।
शुनि चैव श्वपाके च पण्डिताः समदर्शिनः ॥

*vidhya-vinay-sampanne
brahmane gavi hastini
shuni chaiva shva-pake cha
panditah sama-darshinah*

The humble sages, because of accurate knowledge, see with equality of vision, a learned and gentle brahmin, a cow, an elephant, a dog and a dog-eater [outcaste]. -Sri Bhagavad Gita Ch.5; V.18.

इहैव तैर्जितः सर्गो येषां साम्ये स्थितं मनः ।
निर्दोषं हि समं ब्रह्म तस्माद्ब्रह्मणि ते स्थिताः ॥

*ihaiva tairjitah sargo
yesham samye sthitam manah
nirdosham hi samam brahma
tasmad brahmani te sthitah*

Those whose minds get established in sameness and equanimity have already conquered the conditions of birth and death. They are flawless like Brahman, and thus they are already into Brahman. -Sri Bhagavad Gita Ch.5; V. 19.

आत्मौपम्येन सर्वत्र समं पश्यति योऽर्जुन ।
सुखं वा यदि वा दुःखं स योगी परमो मतः ॥

*atmaup-amyena sarvatra
samam pashyati yorjuna
sukham va yadi va dukham
sa yogi paramo matah*

He is a perfect yogi who, by comparison to his own self, sees the true equality of all beings, in both their happiness and their distress, O Arjuna! - Sri Bhagavad Gita Ch.6; V.32.

समोऽहं सर्वभूतेषु न मे द्वेष्योऽस्ति न प्रियः ।
ये भजन्ति तु मां भक्त्या मयि ते तेषु चाप्यहम् ॥

samoham sarva-bhuteshu
na me dveshyosti na priyah
ye bhajanti tu mam bhaktya
mayi te teshu chapyaham

I envy no one, nor am I partial to anyone. I am equal to all, but whoever renders service unto Me in devotion is a friend, is in Me, and I am also a friend to him. -Sri Bhagavad Gita Ch.9; V.29.

Learning from the scriptures

A consciously awakened person does not distinguish between species or castes. This is because of their relationship to the Supreme.

Equanimity of mind is the sign of self-realization. We should consider those who have actually attained such a stage to have conquered material conditions, specifically birth and death. As long as one identifies with this body, he is considered a conditioned soul, but as soon as one is elevated to the stage of equanimity through realization of self, he gets liberated from conditional life. One is no longer subject to take birth in the material world, but can enter the spiritual sky after death.

One who becomes consciously awakened is a perfect *yogi;* he is aware of everyone's happiness and distress by dint of his own personal experience.

The cause of the distress of a living entity is forgetfulness of his relationship with God.

One may question here that if God is equal to everyone, and no one is His special friend, then why does He take a special interest in the devotees who are always engaged in His transcendental service? But this is not discrimination; it is natural. It may orient any man in this material world towards charity, yet he has a special interest in his own children.

How to curb discrimination?

1. **Education**–Education alone is the biggest alleviator of human kind. It not only gives us a perspective of fairness and equanimity, but also helps us understand the divisive politics of fear. The more you educate people around you, the better you can contribute towards eradication of discrimination.

2. **Revise the standards**–Certain standard of measurement are very skewed. For example, the over-rated virtue of fairness of skin or the parameters of body contours at the beauty pageant contests. There should not be a standard measure to evaluate humans in comparison with one another. Instead, respect their uniqueness and individuality.

3. **Change the Mind-set** - As you grew up, the surrounding society rubbed certain discriminatory practices on to you. Now that you are grown up and educated, the onus is on you to bring a change.

4. **Superiority Complex**–Most discriminatory practices spring out of a superiority complex. Are you always trying to be the first among equals? Do you have a swelling ego? Do you look down upon others with pity? Check your

emotions before they assume huge proportions and manifest as hatred.

5. **Engage appropriately**–Every finger in the hand can perform one distinct function better. Likewise, every human can perform some distinct activity better. Identify their potential and deploy them for a specific role they are good at. This will instil confidence and dignity in the person while performing that job.

The aircraft story

Once a white South African lady found herself sitting next to a black man in a British Airways aircraft from Johannesburg. She called the cabin crew to complain about her seating. She demanded her seat to be changed because she couldn't be seated next to that man.

The stewardess said that the flight was fully occupied but she would try. Soon she returned and said: "I've checked but the economy seats are full. I've spoken to the cabin services director, and the club is also full. However, we do have one seat in the first class."

Before the lady could react to this, the stewardess continued,

"It is most extraordinary to make this kind of upgrade, but in the given circumstances, the captain felt that it was outrageous that someone be forced to sit next to such an obnoxious person."

With that, she turned to the black man and said, "so if you'd like to get your things sir, I have a first class seat ready for you."

Now this man got an ovation from all the other passengers in the plane as he walked towards the front of the plane.

"Wind does not discriminate—it touches everyone, everything. HE liked that about wind."
– Lish McBride, Necromancing the Stone.

Chapter 11: ZEAL OVER LAZINESS

What is laziness?

Laziness is the dis-inclination to work or perform an action despite being capable of doing so. It is primarily a low self-esteem stemming from low self-confidence.

Laziness can also result out of your disbelief in the activity's outcome or your lack of interest in it. Lack of motivation is another cause for laziness.

Boredom is a situation which arises out of being dis-interested in the work you do or can do and hence results in laziness. Tchaikovsky said: "Inspiration is a guest that does not willingly visit the lazy."

Types of laziness
There are three types of laziness.
1. Comfort oriented
2. Loss of heart
3. Indifference

Let us understand the three types of laziness.
1. **Comfort oriented** – When the mind is a comfort seeker, one tries to always stay cozy in their comfort zone. If any action requires them to step out of their comfort zone, they sulk and avoid any inconvenience.
2. **Loss of heart** – It is a type of laziness with feelings like 'why me?'... 'poor me!'. One could sit in front of the laptop and watch one webseries after the other or turn on the Netflix watching one movie after the other. They just cannot get started with some meaningful assignment because they are never enthused enough for any activity.

3. **Indifference** – While the above example of loss of heart is a bit about vulnerability, the indifferent types couldn't care any less. They are defiant and arrogant. They could binge on eating or drinking or could sleep during any time of the day. If anyone suggests them anything otherwise, they are ready to pick up a fight.

What is procrastination?
Laziness may manifest into procrastination or vacillation or indecision. It is an act of postponing or delaying something. It is a common trait to postpone a task if the deadline is not near. Whether we planned the deliverable for a week or a month, yet action takes place only within the last 12 hours.

While laziness is the inaction to work, procrastination is the choice to do another thing instead.

Here is a short stanza by Gloria Pitzer, which aptly speaks about procrastination.

"*Procrastination is my sin*
It brings me naught but sorrow
I know that I should stop it
In fact, I will -tomorrow"

Wisdom from The Bhagavad Gita about laziness

नियतं कुरु कर्म त्वं कर्म ज्यायो ह्यकर्मणः ।
शरीरयात्रापि च ते न प्रसिद्ध्येदकर्मणः ॥

nityam kuru karma tvam
karma jyayo hy-akarmanah
shareera-yatra-pi cha te
na prasiddhyed-akarmanah

Performing your prescribed duty, the for sake of doing so, is better than inaction. One cannot even maintain one's own physical body with no work. –Sri Bhagavad Gita Ch.3; V.8.

कर्मणैव हि संसिद्धिमास्थिता जनकादयः ।
लोकसङ्ग्रहमेवापि सम्पश्यन्कर्तुमर्हसि ॥

*karman-aiva hi samsiddhim
asthita janakadayah
lok-samgraham-evaapi
sampashyan-katurm-arhasi*

Kings such as Janaka attained perfection solely by performance of prescribed duties. Therefore, just for the sake of educating the people, perform your work. –Sri Bhagavad Gita Ch.3; V.20.

नात्यश्नतस्तु योगोऽस्ति न चैकान्तमनश्नतः ।
न चातिस्वप्नशीलस्य जाग्रतो नैव चार्जुन ॥

*natyashta-astu yogo-sti
na chaikantam-nashnatah
na chati-swapna-sheelasya
jagrato naiva cha-arjuna*

No one can become a yogi, O Arjuna, if one eats too much or eats too little, sleeps too much or does not sleep enough. –Sri Bhagavad Gita Ch.6; V.16.

यदग्रे चानुबन्धे च सुखं मोहनमात्मनः ।
निद्रालस्यप्रमादोत्थं तत्तामसमुदाहृतम् ॥

*yadagre cha-anubandhe cha
sukham mohanam-atmanah
nidralasya-pramodothyam
tat-tamasam-udhahritam*

That happiness which is blind to self-realization, which is delusion from beginning to end and which arises from sleep, laziness and illusion is said to be of the nature of ignorance. –Sri Bhagavad Gita Ch.18; V.39.

Learning from the scriptures

We refer karma to as duty as well as deeds. Hence duty is the action desired of you.

Consistent imperfect actions are better than inaction in pursuit of perfection.

It is hard to even maintain one's body, taking no action. Therefore, action is the minimal force required for anything to move. Do not expect results without performing your duties.

Everyone is at a different wrung of the ladder of evolution in the society and when you have people junior to you or younger than you, they look up to you as their role model. Set an example to them by taking appropriate actions and inspire them.

Lethargy creeps easily into those who either eat too much or too less and in those who sleep too much or too less. Strike the right balance in life. Regulate your sleep, diet and meditation.

Ignorance and delusion about your own duties, not knowing what action they require of you, also leads to laziness.

How to overcome laziness?

1. **Know your deliverables–** maintain a to-do list and know the various deliverables. If you have a written list of things to do, you can begin planning. You would know what needs to be done and by when. Never say you know what is to be done because it's on your mind. That doesn't work. If you don't have your to-do list, you will only end up doing what you get reminded of.

2. **Commit yourself to task**–Check your attitude. Are you a professional or a slacker? A professional person would stick to one's own commitment without sneaking into excuses.

3. **Be answerable to someone**–Find someone to check on you. Make an accountability partner. No accountability and no timeline to deliver can easily trap a person into procrastinating the work until called for.

4. **Improve your self-esteem**–You can work and perform better if you know and believe that the work you do shall add value to this world. If you inculcate self-respect and consider yourself worthy, then you will try to perform to give better results.

5. **Pump up your metabolism (low energy)**–Do you feel sluggish and tired most of the time? If you are physically on a low energy, then it is hard to get up and do anything at all. It is time to work on your lifestyle and regulate your sleep, exercise and diet to unlock your energy through enhanced metabolism.

6. **Motivation**–Do you need someone to motivate, push or prod you for action or are you self-motivated? The key to self-motivation is assuming ownership of the work you do. Once you take charge and consider it your own work rather than a compulsory obligation, then you will be self-motivated. Those who are self–motivated do not easily get trapped in lethargy.

7. **Mindfulness**–You can improve your focus through mindfulness and meditation. Inner illumination comes through meditation. A person who practices meditation gains more inner peace and can guide his/her thoughts into stronger focus. This unlocks the inner energies and drive to take up challenges head on.

8. **Make it interesting**–Dull, boring, repetitive and mundane work or un-interesting

working methods can kill your creativity. Excessive micro-specialisation or division of work can also become boring. Always design a work scope that fulfils your creative needs as well. One must love doing what one does, otherwise who can get motivated to try out anything loathsome? On a lighter note, Robert Heinlein said: *"Progress isn't made by early risers. It's made by lazy men trying to find easier ways to do something."*

9. **Set time-bound Goals**–It is a mere dream if the goals do not have a deadline. Set time-bound goals. Stay committed to it. Share it with your accountability partner as well. Once you have a delivery deadline, you can work out a backward calculation of what needs to be finished by when. You can also smartly determine what needs to be done in this moment and the next.

10. **Fear of failure**–A principal factor for inaction is fear of failure. You develop a fear of failure when you are unsure of the outcome and your mental negativity takes over. "What if I fail? Will I give up or try again? Will I use a unique method or the same?" When you ask yourself these questions, you become more resolute than appalled.

11. **Avoid distractions**–Notifications appearing on the corner of your laptop or the beeps of notification from your mobile phones can distract you endlessly. Mute them all forever. Another form of distraction is a boisterously loud colleague working in an open office. That one noisy cubicle ruins the focus of everyone else. It requires focus of the mind to accomplish any task, hence you must remove the sources of distractions from your vicinity.

Kaizen: Japanese technique to overcome laziness

When people fail to achieve, they tend to give up easily. Masaaki Imai brought the Kaizen technique. Kai = Change and Zen = Wisdom. In this, he suggested a 'one minute' principle for self improvement. If you feel lazy about doing a particular work or adopting a habit, then just do it only for one minute everyday at the same time. It should seem easy. Right? In most parts of the world it is believed that enormous amount of efforts is required to achieve anything. Hence the one-minute principle may seem ineffective but it works. How? You begin with just a minute, but over a period of time, you develop a habit which is addictive. Gradually, you can increase the time span.

"Laziness is nothing more than the habit of resting before you get tired." - Jules Renard

Chapter 12: CAMARDERIE BEATS LONELINESS

What is loneliness?

The need for solitude is not loneliness. Ruskin Bond said: *"You may not enjoy loneliness, because loneliness is sad. But solitude is something else; solitude is what you look forward to when you want to be alone, when you want to be with yourself. So, solitude is something we all need from time to time."*

Loneliness is feeling sad and unhappy about being socially isolated. It makes people feel empty, alone and unwanted. Lonely people are social beings who crave for social contacts, but their state of mind makes it difficult to establish contacts with others. It is a pre-emptive emotional reaction to a perceived isolation.

We all can experience this emotion from time to time, however research says that manifestation of loneliness as a disorder occurs when the feeling of loneliness gets repeated more than twice a week. It is a distressing experience which makes one feel drained out, distracted and upset because they perceive their social interactions much less than desired.

Types of loneliness
There are four types of loneliness:
1. Emotional
2. Social
3. Situational
4. Chronic

Let us understand the four types of loneliness.

1. **Emotional loneliness** – The person understands the lack of love and cause of loneliness. The emotional gap is overbearing.

2. **Social loneliness** – The person is unable to socialise with others because of shyness or sense of social awkwardness.

3. **Situational loneliness** – These are the people who chose to stay and work away from home far from family. Also includes situation when a good friend or family member migrates outside to another town.

4. **Chronic loneliness** – Widowers, people with solo travelling jobs, or those who stayed away from home for a very long period of time, eventually become loners who cannot communicate properly with their family and friends even when they are together.

However, being alone and loneliness aren't the same. We can desire solitude where we choose to be alone to practice a resolute process of gaining peace within. This isn't loneliness because the subject has self-desired for this. Even loneliness never gets imposed upon you by others, but it is your own perception about your lack of human interaction.

Recently, I read an article by Lynn Darling on AARP titled as, 'Is there a medical care for loneliness?' It said that genomic researcher Steve Cole looked at samples of white blood cells (WBC) of lonely people through a molecular microscope. He observed that the blood cells appeared to be in a state of high alert, as if they were confronting a bacterial infection. Hence this was like a disease of loneliness. Louise Hawkley, a senior research scientist at the university of Chicago, made similar pronouncements. She said that there is a human need to be embedded, connected, integrated in a social network.

If loneliness is a disease, then there should be a cure available for it at the pharmacy. If the pain is real, then it should be treatable.

Wisdom from The Bhagavad Gita about loneliness

यो मां पश्यति सर्वत्र सर्वं च मयि पश्यति।
तस्याहं न प्रणश्यामि स च मे न प्रणश्यति॥

yo maam pashyati sarvatra
sarvam cha mayi pashyati
tasyaham na pranashyami
sa cha me na pranashyati

For one who sees Me everywhere and sees everything in Me, I am never lost, nor is he ever lost to Me. -Sri Bhagavad Gita Ch.6; V.30.

समोऽहं सर्वभूतेषु न मे द्वेष्योऽस्ति न प्रिय: ।
ये भजन्ति तु मां भक्त्या मयि ते तेषु चाप्यहम् ॥

samoham sarvabhuteshu
na me dveshyosti na priyah
ye bhajanti tu ma bhaktya
mayi te teshu chapyaham

I envy no one, partial to none. I am equanimous to all, but whoever renders service unto Me in devotion is a friend, is in Me, and I am also a friend to him. -Sri Bhagavad Gita Ch.9; V.29.

बहिरन्तश्च भूतानामचरं चरमेव च ।
सूक्ष्मत्वात्तदविज्ञेयं दूरस्थं चान्तिके च तत् ॥

*bahir-antash-cha bhutanam
acharam charmeva cha
sukshamatva-tad-avigyeyam
durashtam chantike cha tat*

The supreme truth exists within and around all beings. He is subtle; He is beyond the power of the material senses to see or to know. He is far away, yet so near to all. –Sri Bhagavad Gita Ch.13; V.16.

ज्योतिषामपि तज्ज्योतिस्तमसः परमुच्यते ।
ज्ञानं ज्ञेयं ज्ञानगम्यं हृदि सर्वस्य विष्ठितम् ॥

*jyotishaam-api tajjyotis
tamasah param-ucchyate
gyanam gyeyam gyana-gamyam
hridi sarvasya vishishtha-tam*

He is the source of light in all luminous objects. He is beyond the darkness of matter and is un-manifested. He is knowledge; and the object of knowledge, and He is the goal of knowledge. He is situated in everyone's heart. –Sri Bhagavad Gita Ch.13; V.18.

Learning from the scriptures

The one who sees the supreme being as the universe and sees everything in Him is never lost.

Every person in this world has received an equal opportunity to begin with. This universe is impartial to all. Connect yourself with the supreme universal cosmic energy to receive the abundance.

The eternal truth is within us as much as it is all around, and He is beyond the material senses to see and know Him.

He is the source of all illumination, including the light of knowledge.

How to overcome loneliness?

1. **Identify your problem**– Identifying a problem is the first step towards treating it. You know you are lonely if you experience decreased enthusiasm, lack of focus, lack of self-worth, frequent aches and pains, over-doing on stimulants, gazing at TV/ Web shows. Individuals may display several other symptoms according to their experiences.

2. **Socialise**–The first counter attack to loneliness is to socialise. Go out there and meet people, involve with them, engage with them through social activities and gatherings. Do not be judgemental whether or not they are your type. Do not seek perfection because we all are bundles of imperfections. There is a funny side to anyone, try to discover it.

3. **Are you worth their time?** - While we have expectation from others, we must also introspect if we are worth their time. Ask yourself whether you are an interesting person with whom people would be glad to interact? If yes, then a major part of the problem gets sorted out because you don't have to chase them hard, but they will come to seek you instead. Just be exceptional.

4. **Take a lead**- When you are at a gathering, do you wait for people to come and introduce themselves to you or do you reach out to people and introduce yourself? If you take the lead in introducing yourself, you will make friends faster than you think.

5. **Positive Self Talk**–If you keep saying to yourself that you are lonely and this world is not good for you, then you will consciously etch it into your sub-conscious mind with a lot of negativity. Instead, if you are grateful for the

friends you have, you will create a positive self-talk between your conscious and sub-conscious mind and you will have more friends around you.

6. **Hobby**–Pick up any hobby. Practising a hobby is a good way to enjoy your own company while doing something meaningful. Gardening is one such activity where there is some physical labour involved, along-with mental satisfaction of being creative. There are many more hobbies to suit individual preferences.

7. **Be spiritual**–A spiritual person would understand that he is a part of this universe and everything here is related cosmically. As humans, we have the urge to include everyone and everything within us. *All that isn't mine should be mine.* Expand yourself, erase your own boundaries, be inclusive and accept imperfections, merge into this universe.

8. **CBT**- Cognitive Behavioural Therapy helps in treating anxiety, depression, addictions and a variety of other problems presented in counselling and psychotherapy like anger, self-esteem and confidence. All you need to do is to reach out to the right practitioner for help.

My tryst with loneliness

I was living an accomplished life. Great job, loving family, savings in the bank, good health and happiness. I was aiming at self-actualization through training post graduate students on weekends. There was a confident feeling of 'yes! I did it.' I tried to venture into setting up my own business, not once but thrice. As good an intra-preneur I was at work, I repeatedly failed as an entrepreneur. I lost money but gained knowledge and experience in the bargain.

Then a wind blew away my castle made with pack of cards. I lost my job to weird circumstances.

More financial loss and lot of antagonising conditions.

I decided to rebuild myself. I chose to work away from home in a remote location with the sole motivation that the job content was satisfying. It was a far off place with no amenities and very few like minded people around. It took time for me to realise that gradually I slipped into the grip of loneliness and depression. Fortunately, I could sense some early signs of it's manifestation and underwent medical treatment. Timely support from family and colleagues at work helped me to revive.

Suggestions came in from well-wishers that I must join a club or groups of people, play cards, drink something, do something, but it is such a remote place for any of those. I took every opportunity to go out on short excursions, travel and observe. I learnt new things and cultures. I made notes.

Then something turned around. With the help of a mentor, I wrote and published my first book. It went on to become #1 bestseller on Amazon. Inspired by it's success, I wrote two more books. They too became #1 bestsellers.

I was on a roll, so I wanted to write more, like a book every one or two months. I went into a complete recluse to start writing this book. I did not want to get disturbed even by a phone call from home. Then I paused and talked to myself. Hey! why am I pushing myself into the deep dungeons of solitude once again? Writing so many books won't do me any good. There are millions of books out there and who needs one more from me?

I needed to interact with people. So what if I was in a remote location? With all those lockdowns happening, the world is going digital anyway.

I launched my YouTube channel and started interviewing people. Talking to people was a learning and rewarding experience. In this process, they became my friends and we formed a support group. I also became an influencer of books. People send me their books and I summarise and review the books of various authors. It is a different kind of pleasure to celebrate the work and success of others. Soon my YouTube community started growing organically. i.e. I no longer have to invite and request people to subscribe to my channel but they do it because they love the content.

I have a vast experience in the industry, hence I want to share my learnings with people. So within my YouTube channel, I started a segment called 'Lateral Learning.' Here I share some smart tips about business practices and life skills. This should help people and enable me to connect with a larger audience.

Now, I do not have time to sit and ponder. I have a day job where I work full time with complete focus. My time after work, is fully utilised for my other pursuits. So there is no idle mind to turn into a monkey. I don't know where this drive will take me to, but all I know for sure is that now I'm unstoppable.

"Loneliness is my least favourite thing about life. The thing that I'm most worried about is just being alone with nobody to care for or someone who will care for me." –Anne Hathaway.

Chapter 13: HOPE FOR DESPERATE

What is desperation?

Desperation is a condition wherein one has no expectation of anything good or successful to happen. It is a powerful manifestation of negativity that makes a person firmly believe that there is no remedy to him/her problems. One feels not only like a deflated balloon but is also sure that there is a hole in it that prevents it to be inflated again.

A hopeless person loses interest in most things, refrains from activities and events, or avoids contact with people. He/she may no longer value things that might have been once important.

We often associate the feeling of hopelessness with a lack of inspiration and feelings of powerlessness, helplessness, abandonment, captivity, oppression, and isolation. Several studies show that hopelessness is closely linked to poor mental, emotional, and physical health.

Dr. Aaron T. Beck developed The Beck Hopelessness Scale in 1974 by and it became one of the most accepted predictive measures in suicide risk assessment. Many prospective and retrospective studies found that suicide risk could get predicted more reliably based on hopelessness than by the seriousness of depression only.

Types of despair

There are nine types of despair. Let us understand each of them.

1. **Lack of inspiration** – The uninspired feeling when one doesn't see any opportunity for growth and stops using creativity.

2. **Powerless** – Feels lack of control over one's own life. Submits to the will of others. Incapable of taking charge of own life.

3. **Alienation** – Doesn't feel oneself as a part of the community. The constant feeling of being an outsider.

4. **Oppressed** – Feeling socially, racially discriminated and looked down upon.

5. **Foresaken** – Feeling abandoned. Unable to seek help from anyone.

6. **Unsafe** – Feeling unsafe in the environment. Unable to make oneself comfortable with people around. Everyone feels like an enemy.

7. **Captive** – Feeling stuck in an abusive or toxic relationship. Unable to find courage to break free.

8. **Limitedness** – Personal skills are ignored or cannot be used. Bound with prescribed rules to follow.

9. **Doomed** – The end is near, kind of feeling. One feels trapped in a hostile situation. A gloomy feeling that only death can end this situation.

I came across a poem by Alicia Strong which she titles as 'Hopelessness':

> I look in the mirror
> and what do I see?
> Bitter disappointment
> staring back at me.
>
> It seems no matter
> what I do,
> I just can't seem
> to get through to you.
>
> I'm clawing away
> at what's left of me.
> and people won't let

the pieces be.

I shed those pieces for a reason.
I'm sick of being stuck in this rainy season.
Walking around with a cloud above my head.
Sometimes I think I'd much rather be dead.
Sometimes...

Wisdom from The Bhagavad Gita about desperation

ये यथा मां प्रपद्यन्ते तांस्तथैव भजाम्यहम् ।

मम वर्त्मान वर्तन्ते मनुष्याः पार्थ सर्वशः ॥

ye yatha maam prap-adhyante
tams-tathaiva bhajamyaham
mum vartamaan vartante
manushyah partha sarvashah

As they surrender unto Me, I reward them accordingly. Everyone follows My path, O Partha. – Sri Bhagavad Gita Ch.4; V.11.

अनन्याश्चिन्तयन्तो मां ये जनाः पर्युपासते ।

तेषां नित्याभियुक्तानां योगक्षेमं वहाम्यहम् ॥

ananya-ashchinta-yanto maam
ye janah payurpaste
tesham nitya-bhiyuktanam
yoga-khshema vahamyaham

Those who always worship Me with exclusive devotion, and meditate on My transcendental form; to them I grant what they lack, and I preserve what they have. –Sri Bhagavad Gita Ch.9; V.22.

मन्मना भव मद्भक्तो मद्याजी मां नमस्कुरु ।

मामेवैष्यसि युक्त्वैवमात्मानं मत्परायणः ॥

manmana bhav mudbhakto
madhyaji maam namaskuru
mamevaish-yasi yukt-vaivam-
atmanam mat-parayanah

Always engage your mind in My thoughts. Be devoted to Me; Offer obeisance to Me and worship Me. You will surely come to Me if you get completely immersed in Me. -Sri Bhagavad Gita Ch.9; V.34.

सर्वधर्मान्परित्यज्य मामेकं शरणं व्रज ।
अहं त्वां सर्वपापेभ्यो मोक्षयिष्यामि मा शुच: ॥

sarva-dharmaan-paritajya
maamekam sharanam vraja
aham tvaam sarva-papebhyo-
mokshyish-yami ma shuchah

Shun all religions and just surrender to Me. I shall absolve you from all sin. Do not worry. –Sri Bhagavad Gita Ch.18; V.66.

यत्र योगेश्वर: कृष्णो यत्र पार्थो धनुर्धर: ।
तत्र श्रीर्विजयो भूतिर्ध्रुवा नीतिर्मतिर्मम ॥ ७८ ॥

yatra yogeshwarah krishno
yatra partho dhanur-dharah
tatra shrivijayo bhutir-
Dhruva nitir-matir-mama

Wherever there are omni-potent Krishna and Arjuna, the great archer, there will certainly be opulence, victory, extraordinary power, and morality. –Sri Bhagavad Gita Ch.18; V.78.

सहजं कर्म कौन्तेय सदोषमपि न त्यजेत् ।
सर्वारम्भा हि दोषेण धूमेनाग्निरिवावृता: ॥

sahajam karma kaunteya

> *sa-dosham-api na tyajet*
> *sarvarambha hi doshena*
> *dhumen-agnir ivaavritah*

One should perform one's duty, O son of Kunti, even if such karma is full of imperfect actions. Every karma may get shadowed by a flaw, like glowing fire gets engulfed in smoke. –Sri Bhagavad Gita Ch.18; V.48.

Learning from the scriptures

Giving up your self-ego to connect with the supreme, and walking the divine path raises the hope of the devoted person to attain liberation. When you believe in yourself, you shall gain confidence and wisdom.

Those immersed in their beliefs and devotion to the supreme do not fail in their aim because He carries along those truly devoted to Him. When your objectives are defined well, you minimise the chances of failure.

Negative thoughts fearing an unpleasant outcome manifests itself in failure. Positive affirmations ensure success because the thoughts that prevail upon your mind all the time through your conscious awareness, have the power to write them upon the layers of your sub-conscious mind.

The core essential knowledge about the supreme super cedes the knowledge of rituals and religious processes. Be pro-active instead of reactive. Understand the wisdom behind your actions instead of following some rules that you do not fully understand.

Righteousness prevails over might. When your thoughts and actions are ethical and aimed at larger benefit for all, your hopes for success shall soar high.

A person may be good at certain core skills, but lack of motivation for any reason can make him/her dispirited for action.

In the scheme of universal motion, there are wheels within wheels and every gear has to move in tandem with others. Hence, the need to perform duty in inevitable.

The consciously aware people understand the universe has a purpose and a plan, and every individual has to follow the master-plan.

Your scope of duties shall demand certain actions from you. Perform them, even though with imperfections. Do not succumb to inaction in pursuit of perfection.

When a consciously aware person is in sync with the cosmic supreme, success and ethics get assured.

How to give hope for curing desperation?

1) **Understand the root cause of the problem**–Any problem is easier to deal with if the cause gets known. Are you hopeless because of sudden loss of job? Loss of relationship? Or a setback in educational pursuit? Try to introspect and analyse the cause. Give it a thought and identify the root cause of the problem.

2) **Inner happiness**–Inner happiness cannot come from outer sources. A meditative person who walks the path of self-awakening and self-awareness understands the difference between the inner and the outer world. Any external reward or comfort has a temporary impact, but inner happiness prevails sustainably.

3) **Gratitude** - Find gratitude in small things. Often life is full of abundance, but we cannot express gratitude for small things because we are waiting for a big blast to happen. It is our thanklessness that makes us hopeless more than any lack of hope.

4) **Do that One thing** - Find one thing that only you can do and then experience the pleasure of doing it. You will feel the satisfaction of adding value and enhancing your self-worth. We must focus on that one most important thing required to be done at that point in time to prevail over the situation. For example, they locked the world down in 2020 because of a global catastrophe. People watched daily news and tracked the number of cases, only to get terrified. The wise ones upgraded their skills through online courses and discovered alternative profession like digital coaching / learning. They did that one thing which was required to keep their hopes alive, and several new start-ups emerged as businesses were shutting down. Once the news media stopped broadcasting the numbers, people went back to work.

5) **Set small and achievable goals**– When hopes are running low, set small and achievable goals. Achieve them and feel satisfied. When starting a new venture, take a smaller project for testing out the learning curve. Let the first project not be humongous and equivalent to alleviation of world hunger. Are your goals achievable or too big to accomplish? Have you bitten more than you can chew? Have you taken up too many assignments at a time and are getting overwhelmed? Are you facing a burnout? I am not advocating a complacent life. It is good to work hard and be a multi-tasker. Browning-up is good for you to have a flavourful life, but beware of a burnout. Keep your goals practical and achievable.

The joy of achieving one minor success motivates us to take up another challenge.

6) **Find a purpose in life** - Do you have clarity about what you want in life? Life without purposefulness is like a driftwood floating downstream. One could flow, but without knowing where they are heading to. When you know what to expect from life, then you are more likely to have a set of goals to achieve. You are less likely to drift away when you have a set of goals and deadlines before you. Hence, it is important to chart out the path of your life. Iterations in the plan are inevitable, but it is imperative to have a basic plan at the outset.

7) **Doing things for a right reason**–Have you met people who are employed in some business but still feel they aren't doing what they are supposed to? They are living from one paycheck to another paycheck, but ignoring their calling.

He is a lion in a birdcage,
A bird deep under the sea,
He is doing what best he could,
But he isn't where he ought to be.

Ask yourself whether you are working just for earning that salary or for passion? Not everyone is fortunate enough to work for their passion, because most people never discover their calling. Even if they do sense a calling, they aren't ready to break their comfort zone and strive to achieve what they want. Resultantly, they drag themselves unwillingly through whatever they get handed out with, and keep doing it unwillingly in a loathsome way. Have the courage to break free from your own inhibitions and pursue what excites you.

8) **Fearfulness kills motivation**– Fear of failure is one of the biggest factors for demotivation or dispiritedness. What if...? We can frame many questions with the phrase 'what if.' Draw a decision tree with the phrase 'what if' then there would be two branches. One leading to success and another leading to failure. To remain fixated on the prospect of failure will always prevent you from taking the first step ahead.

9) **Undermining self**–Are you a victim of self-sabotage? Thinking you are not capable or worthy of doing something weighs you down with your own negative perception about self. Feeling left out, *"Oh! I could have done more, but time has moved on."* Unable to cope with the pace makes you more dispirited against action. Believe in yourself that you are more capable than you think. Refrain from self criticism and give a shot to action. One step towards action is better than ten plans in the mind.

10) **Conflict of values**–It is hard for most people to change their profession if required. If you are an engineer, can you become a teacher? Dignity of labour is something hard to appreciate. We have our fixed mind-sets against venturing into another field. Trying out some new start-up venture meets its first resistance within self. A person who has retired as a CEO of a corporate would rather sit idle after retirement than open up a pizza outlet or a coffee shop. Maybe financially there is no need to work, but the conflict of values comes first.

11) **Lack of challenges**–Do you perform better under pressure or deadline? Some jobs have more sharp deadlines, while others are complacent. Performance is sub-optimal, where answerability is low. Always put yourself into a challenging environment where you may not lie back and daydream. Surround yourself with action

oriented work and be in the company of people who can question your actions or inactions.

12) **Mental issues**–People who are already suffering from mental issues like loneliness, grief, depression, are more likely to be dispirited for any action. Mental issues have to gain importance as a medical condition and must get treated clinically.

13) **Eat natural food**–Desperation triggers hormonal and biological disorder. During this phase, eat natural and easily digestible food. Processed and industrially manufactured food products are never good for the body. They are even worse when you are feeling hopeless because the body is weak inside.

14) **Avoid intoxicants**–We often see that people resort to drinking or substance misuse when they are hopeless. These things only worsen their condition and push them into a deeper depression. Inebriated condition pushes people more towards suicide because they lose their mental balance to judge what is right.

15) **Meet a therapist**–When the body temperature rises by one degree, we admit there is some illness. However, when there is inner pain, we often ignore it. Admit that inner pain of the mind is also an illness which requires medical attention. Meet a therapist to begin with so that he/she may administer cognitive behavioural therapy.

Why desperation despite a fulfilled life?

Ali McCloskey in her talk at TEDx Bath University made a candid revelation about her life. She had a successful career in banking for 13 years.

She says that in our lives there are two levels of fulfilment. The immediate short term fulfilment and the permanent long term fulfilment. Apparently, she was into a successful career in terms of wealth and recognition but she lacked in her fulfilment from her family life. She got dispirited to go back to work. Her desperation was despite her success because her success was not congruent with her values.

After two weeks of soul searching she realised that she valued her family more than her job. She quit her successful banking job to start her own Pilates and Fitness business. Further she found her zone into helping people and trained herself as a life coach, studying NLP/TLT and hypnosis. She got herself to work with couples in the area of work and relationships.

She puts across several introspective questions for us to ponder. What will become of us if we settle for a life of mediocrity rather than dare to ask for, or expect more than we've been conditioned for? What is it that we need to do in order to create a life of meaning? What happens if we don't plan and take an active part in designing and orchestrating our lives? If we don't, no one else will.

"To hope means to be ready at every moment for that which is not yet born, and yet not become desperate if there is no birth in our lifetime." - Erich Fromm

Chapter 14: RESISTANCE TO TEMPTATION

What is temptation?

Temptation is a desire to engage in short-term urges for enjoyment that threaten long-term goals. These urges are mostly something wrong, unwise or unethical. The ancient texts in India have a word *Kaama* which means physiological needs like food, sex, comforts etc. Kaama is one of the four major pursuits in life, namely Artha (material), Dharma (spiritual), Kaama (physiological) and Moksha (renunciation).

In a broader sense, if the sight of delicious food tempts you to eat it, then it is not such a sinister temptation, however, the cravings to gorge excessively because of gluttony and the desire to experience unscrupulous 'Taamsik' food and beverages is a temptation. Desire to steal is temptation. Desiring sex with spouse for mutual and spiritual bonding is not temptation, but desiring any physical relation with a person outside your marriage as a lustful pleasure seeker is temptation. Sometimes it is not just a self-desire but the opportunity to grow, receive benefits and rewards by collaborating, also leads to temptation.

The impact of temptation can influence the health and well-being of the person. Indulgence would destroy his/her moral fabric, and abstinence causes stress and anxiety because of unfulfilled desires. Wise people across time have professed that immoral and illicit act gets conducted not by the compulsion of the parts of the body or by the person physically, but it is first purported into the mind of the person. The mind is the controller of the body and its actions.

Oscar Wilde said: *"The only way to get rid of temptation is to yield to it... I can resist everything but temptation."*

There are many similar theories based on misbeliefs that one can just for once indulge and get over with the temptation in the future. Osho (Acharya Rajneesh) advocated in favour of mutual gratification with no strings attached to get over with temptation, but the reality differs from what got purported. Nobody actually gets over with it easily.

Two monks and a girl

Here is a story to understand how to keep something off your mind. Two monks were walking through a forest. Around dusk they saw a young girl writhing in pain and unable to walk because she injured her ankle. She had come there to fetch firewood and she fell off a tree. One of them offered to lift her and help her reach her home. The other monk felt disturbed, but obeyed the senior and lifted the bundle of twigs while his mate lifted the girl in his arms. No one spoke during the journey. Once they crossed the forest, they left the girl and her bundle of twigs at the doorstep of her hut and continued walking. After walking a few miles, the senior monk noticed his colleague felt disturbed, so he started a conversation.

"We practice celibacy, so why did you touch a girl? This act will incite the sinister temptation in you?" the junior monk complained to lighten his heavy heart.

"I just helped a human being in dire need, and I left her right there at her home. We have come ahead several miles, but I see you are still carrying her burden in your mind," replied the monk.

This conversation teaches us how temptation is deep-seated in our minds and how difficult it is to overcome the vexation.

Types of temptation
Temptation are of three types.
1. Hedonism
2. Egoism
3. Materialism

Let us understand the three types of temptation.

1. **Hedonism** – This is the temptation for satisfaction of hunger and lust. These are physiological temptations for pleasure. These are instinctive, related to the carnal desires and pleasures of the flesh.

2. **Egoism** – This is the temptation to exercise control over other people to feed the ego and might. These are matter of pride.

3. **Materialism** – This is the temptation to have control over maximum wealth and resources. The more the merrier is the belief as abundance of wealth provides a feeling of security.

Wisdom from the Bhagavad Gita about temptation

यततो ह्यपि कौन्तेय पुरुषस्य विपिश्चतिः ।
इन्द्रियाणि प्रमाथीनि हरन्ति प्रसभं मनः ॥

yatato hyapi kaunteya
purushasya vipakshitah
indriyani pramathini

haranti prasambham manah

The senses are strong and impetuous, O Arjuna. They forcibly carry away the mind even of a man of discretion, who endeavours to control them. –Sri Bhagavad Gita Ch.2; V.60.

तानि सर्वाणि संयम्य युक्त आसीत मत्परः ।
वशे हि यस्येन्द्रियाणि तस्य प्रज्ञा प्रतिष्ठिता ॥

*taani sarvaani samyamya
yukta aseeta matparah
vashe hi yasyendriyani
tasya pragyaa pratishthita*

One who practices restraint and controls his senses, and is conscious of God, is as a person of steadfast intelligence. –Sri Bhagavad Gita Ch.2; V.61.

आपूर्यमाणमचलप्रतिष्ठं
समुद्रमापः प्रविशन्ति यद्वत् ।
तद्वत्कामा यं प्रविशन्ति सर्वे
स शान्तिमाप्नोति न कामकामी ॥

*apoorya-manam-achala-pratishtham
samudram-apah pravishanti yadvat
tadvat-kama yam pravishanti sarve
say shantim-apnoti na kama-kami*

A person who does not get flustered by the incessant flow of desires; like ocean that consumes the rivers, ever being filled yet remains still; can alone achieve peace, and not the person who strives to satiate such desires. –Sri Bhagavad Gita Ch.2; V.70.

दैवी ह्येषा गुणमयी मम माया दुरत्यया ।
मामेव ये प्रपद्यन्ते मायामेतां तरन्ति ते ॥

daivī hy eṣā guṇa-mayī
mama māyā duratyayā
mām eva ye prapadyante
māyām etāṁ taranti te

This divinity comprising three modes of materiality is hard to overcome. Three are, of goodness (sattva), passion (rajas) and ignorance (tamas). Those who have surrendered unto God can easily cross beyond them. -Sri Bhagavad Gita Ch.7; V.14.

Learning from the scriptures

Even the most resolute people who tried to conquer their senses got tricked and tempted into indulgence. Hermit sage Vishwamitra was very resolute in pursuit of great supernatural powers, but he succumbed to the charms of seductress celestial nymph Menaka.

The five senses (sight, sound, smell, taste and touch) are like five powerful horses that drive our body, which is just like a chariot in which our soul undertakes the journey of life. You can ride the chariot of your life if you can reign in the horses and keep them under your control. Uncontrolled senses would gallop into the oblivion, take you away from the mainstream.

The ocean remains calm despite several rivers merging into it. Such calm and composed person alone can attain peace. Attaining peace is difficult for the flustered person, who does not have control over his/her senses.

The three Gunas are the basic state of mind of a person according to which one conducts his/her life. **Sattva guna is goodness and** compassion. Rajas or *'rajo guna'* is a passion for pleasure. Tamas, or *'tamo guna'* is ignorant, selfish and carnal.

This concept requires a better understanding hence here are two examples. The first example is about food. Sattva person eats nutritious food essential for the body and health, Rajas person eats scrumptious rich food for pleasure and taste, while the Tamas person eats unhealthy food and drinks intoxicants to feed the devil inside.

The second example is about their behaviour. If there is a fire in the building they are working in, the Tamas person gets panicky, yells and screams for help, the Rajas person will find the nearest exit to save his/her own life, while the Sattva person will look for a fire extinguisher around to douse the fire. These examples help us identify the nature of ourselves and others around.

How to resist temptation?

Here are some ways to tackle the problem in its roots and get rid of it.

1. **Blame it on your hormones–** There are certain hormones in our body which push us into doing certain activities. It is not you, but your hormones acting up against you and make you crave for something. We have to observe what triggers those hormones. What are the sources of influence that trigger the temptation? So the first step is identifying the cause-and-effect relationship. Does watching porn make you irresistibly excited? If yes, then stop watching it. Does interacting with a particular person urge you to touch or get too close to that person? If yes, then limit your access

to the source and wait till the thoughts blow away from your mind.

2. **Do not act cool**–If you choose to remain a non-smoker, then why hang around in the sit out where a bunch of guys who are smoking? Repeated exposure to passive smoking will draw you into it. Do not flirt even remotely with anyone if you do not intend to start off an extra-marital affair. It needs a strong personal character and will to make your own choice to say No!

3. **Know the consequences**–Seek the truth. You should know and understand the consequences of your acts of indulgence. Think about its impact on your health, reputation, family, and relationships. Once you know what you have got to lose in the bargain for your indulgence, chances are better that you will make an informed choice.

4. **Respond but do not react**–To react is like running away from something. When you try to run away from temptations, they chase you even more. To respond is a mature, well-informed choice that you have made. Take your time to talk to yourself. Make a self-report to note down your trigger points and work out a plan on how to limit the access to them. My office colleagues used to party out once in a few months. The frequency increased. It was coming down to every weekend. I wasn't comfortable with this and I had to opt out. So I enrolled myself in a professional enhancement course which had contact classes every weekend. I explained the scenario to my colleagues, who understood my position with compassion. Now, this was my response to temptation.

5. **Use distraction method**–Temptation is a mind game. There is more impulsiveness in the mind than in the body. Distract your mind by regular walks, yoga and

meditation. These are a few simple techniques, easy to learn and perform. They have other consequential benefits too, besides pre-empting the mind going astray.

6. **Healthy diet plan**–Adopt and follow a healthy diet plan which not only supports physical health but also helps build a balanced mind. I am from a place where late night wedding parties are commonplace. I prefer eating early. If I eat late at parties, close to midnight, I get digestive issues. So I found my hack. I have my early dinner at home as usual and then go to attend the party. I meet and greet everyone, holding a glass in hand. Nobody notices whether I ate, and once the meeting and greeting gets done, I quietly leave. I find it a cool idea that works for me.

7. **Build a confidante**–Have a friend who checks you. Let him stop you from having another beer or another cigarette. Keep those friends close who can scold you and punish you. My son's classmate stole money from his dad's wallet to date a girlfriend. His Mom asked my son the truth and he revealed the story. He also chided his friend. Two years later, while leaving school, the friend acknowledged with gratitude for having checked him that day. This changed his course of life and got him more inclined towards his career.

8. **Apps to track habits**–Install some apps to track your habits like walking, sleeping, exercise and calorie intake. Smart watch and aura rings are cool devices. They passively help you with a self-report without making your details public. Begin with a pedometer to count the number of steps you walk every day. Whatever you measure can get optimised.

9. **Opt for a lesser evil**–Pick something that is a lesser evil than what is tempting you. A nicotine vaporiser instead of a

cigarette, a mock-tail instead of a cocktail, self-gratification instead of violating someone.

10. **Change the peg**–Here, peg is not a glass of your favourite drink but a wooden peg that is used in place of nails to hold your wooden furniture. In olden days, when iron nails were not invented, bamboo splinters or pegs were used to keep the furniture together. They hammered another fresh peg through it when it decayed or got worn out. Change the peg means replace an addictive habit with a new one. I got addicted to gulping a large mug of black coffee every hour. I knew I had to cut it down to two a day, but how? I changed the peg. I bought an electric kettle to heat water, and whenever I had the urge for another coffee, I took a mug full of boiling water and sipped it until the last. Initially, I felt weird, but gradually this new habit took over. It actually helped me to cut down on coffee.

11. **The inner voice**–You know that temptation is an inner lie and you shouldn't indulge. The angel inside you checks you in a feeble voice, but the devil in you coaxes you in a gruff overtone. To whom would you listen? I would rather leave this question for you to answer.

How to face temptation?

Answer these questions to yourself honestly. Did you ever feel tempted? Did you try to resist temptation? Did you ever cross your resistence and gave in to your temptation? Did you experience that the more you tried to resit a temptation, the harder it became to resist? If your answer to all these questions is 'yes' then you are absolutely a normal human being.

The mind always thinks about those things you tell it not to think about. Who decides for you what is forbidden and what is not? Why was it a sin for Adam and Eve to bite into an apple? What else could have been the purpose of their life, just wandering around the heaven without interacting with each other? Are we humans really an outcome of their sin or are we in the process of evolving from lower beings to higher beings?

What comes to you as a natural instinct cannot be avoided or controlled forever. Every indulgence should not push you into the guilt of having sinned. The only way to ensure that your decisions for your actions are good or not, is that you must gain inner awareness to take those decisions that are good for you and for the people around you. When there is a doubt about the righteousness of an action, it probably requires detailed reasoning. When the mind is unsure of doing something, it is your inner voice telling you to introspect before you act.

"Do not worry about avoiding temptation. As you grow older, it will avoid you." -Joey Adams.

Chapter 15: CHASTITY FROM SINFULNESS

What is sinfulness?

Sinfulness is failing to adhere to moral principles and indulging in unsocial activities that are considered by the society as sinful. Chastity vs sinfulness, right vs wrong, pious vs impure and the like, are definitions that keep changing across time. What they once considered a sin becomes a new normal in another time and place. It can vary between civilisations and cultures.

At one time, it was a virtue for a widow to self-immolate herself on the pyre of her husband to become a 'sati'. It is no longer a virtue, but we see perpetrators of this ritual as criminals.

This is the impact of evolvement of morality across time. In some eastern and middle eastern cultures, it is a taboo to have a physical relationship outside marriage, whereas, in other parts of the world, it is a very common social practice. This is an example of a geographic difference in cultures and their morality.

The world is more interconnected now than ever, and exchange of cultures is faster. Both east and west are learning from each other and picking out key takeaways from each other, their cultures and beliefs.

We are talking about Bhagavad Gita and the vast knowledge in its hymns and verses. There are other cultures as well that share similar views about sins and morality. Interacting with people and talking to them helps us know them better.

Wisdom from The Bhagavad Gita about sinfulness

अपि चेदसि पापेभ्यः सर्वेभ्यः पापकृत्तमः ।
सर्वं ज्ञानप्लवेनैव वृजिनं सन्तरिष्यसि ॥

*api chedasi paapebhyah
sarve-bhyah papa-krit-tamah
sarva gyana-plaven-aiva
vrijinam santarish-yashi*

Even the most sinful of all sinners will be able to cross the ocean of miseries while sailing in the boat of transcendental knowledge. –Sri Bhagavad Gita Ch.4; V.36.

यथैधांसि समिद्धोऽग्निर्भस्मसात्कुरुतेऽर्जुन ।
ज्ञानाग्निः सर्वकर्माणि भस्मसात्कुरुते तथा ॥

*yathai-dhaamsi samiddhognir
bhasma-sat-kurute-arjuna
gyan-agnih sarva-karmani
bhasma-saat-kurute tahtaa*

O Arjuna, the fire of knowledge burns to ashes all materialistic activities, like a blazing fire that turns firewood to ashes. -Sri Bhagavad Gita Ch.4; V.37.

ब्रह्मण्याधाय कर्माणि सङ्गं त्यक्त्वा करोति यः ।
लिप्यते न स पापेन पद्मपत्रमिवाम्भसा ॥

*brahman-adhyaya karmani
sangam-tyaktvaa karotiyah
lipyate na sa papena
Padma-patram-ivaam-bhasa*

One who performs his duty without getting attached to the karma, surrendering the results unto the Supreme Lord, is unaffected by sinful action, just as the lotus leaf is untouched by water around it. –Sri Bhagavad Gita Ch.5; V.10.

अपि चेत्सुदुराचारो भजते मामनन्यभाक् ।
साधुरेव स मन्तव्य: सम्यग्व्यवसितो हि स: ॥

api chet-su-duracharo
bhajate mamanya-bhaak
sadhur-ev sa mantavyah
samagya-vyavasito hi saha

Even if one commits the most abominable action, he can hope for absolution if he is engaged in devotional service and is sincerely pursuing in his determination. –Sri Bhagavad Gita Ch.9; V.30.

यो मामजमनादिं च वेत्ति लोकमहेश्वरम् ।
असम्मूढ: स मर्त्येषु सर्वपापै: प्रमुच्यते ॥

yo maam-ajam-anadim cha
vetti loka-maheshwaram
asammudhah sa martyeshu
sarva-papeah pramuchhyate

He who knows God as the unborn, as the eternal, as the Supreme Lord of all the worlds; only the one, undeluded among people, gets freed from all sins. –Sri Bhagavad Gita Ch.10; V.3.

तत्र सत्त्वं निर्मलत्वात्प्रकाशकमनामयम् ।
सुखसङ्गेन बध्नाति ज्ञानसङ्गेन चानघ ॥

tatra sattvam nirmal-atvaat
prakashakam-anamayam
sukha-ssangena badhnaati
gyana-sangena chanagha

O sinless one, the path of piety, of being purer than any other, is illuminating, and it frees one from all sinful reactions. Those who follow the path of piety become conditioned by a sense of happiness and knowledge. –Sri Bhagavad Gita Ch.14; V.6.

सर्वधर्मान्परित्यज्य मामेकं शरणं व्रज ।
अहं त्वां सर्वपापेभ्यो मोक्षयिष्यामि मा शुच: ॥

sarva-dharman-parityajya
mamekam sharanam vraja
aham tvaam sarva-papebhyo
moksh-yishyami ma shuchah

Abandon all forms of religion and just surrender to the supreme being. Only He shall deliver you from all sinful reactions. –Sri Bhagavad Gita Ch.18; V.66.

Learning from the scriptures

Even a sinner can hope to be chastised if he/she takes to the path of self-realization and self-consciousness. The flame of knowledge annihilates the sinister impurities just as fire burns dead wood into ashes.

A soldier has to kill the opponent. A judge has to pass a death sentence to a condemned criminal. They are merely performing their duties to the nation, hence not attached to these karmas. It is just like a lotus flower that grows in water yet untouched by it.

One who takes to the path of devotion to the supreme gets absolved of sins. Hence the consequences of life are futuristic and it gives you a chance to leave the past behind to create a clean future ahead.

One who takes to the path of self-realization is several rungs higher on the ladder of evolution. However, God is not to be misunderstood as a human who walked this earth in history but as a supreme cosmic energy that always existed and shall remain through eternity.

Happiness and the wisdom of knowledge get experienced by those who walk the path of piety.

Religions and rituals are not the right path to God. Connect yourself directly with the creator. Only He can help you attain salvation.

How to avoid sinning and get chastised against sin?

There are two aspects to understand here.

First, it requires what sort of action to help you against sin? One is a preventive action, and the other is corrective action.

Second, what causes you to commit a sin? As discussed prior in the introduction to this book, there are six principle vices that tarnish our soul. *Kama* (lust), *Krodha* (anger), *Madha* (ego), *Lobha* (greed), *Moha* (attachment), *Matsarya* (jealousy). The predominance of anyone or more of these vices provokes a person to commit a sin.

Whenever you feel you are on the wrong path, or if you ever wonder whether what you are doing is right, then please know it is your inner conscience questioning you and warning you. If you listen to your own inner voice and change the course of your life, then you may consider yourself as a consciously aware person who doesn't easily get tarnished by sin.

If someone close to you (a friend or a family member) questions you and checks your wrongdoing, then you are lucky to be in the company of good people around you who can help to prevent you from walking the wrong path.

The next level of check comes from enforcement. For example, if you are eyeing someone or making flirtatious advances towards someone and then you get confronted by someone (maybe her friend or relative or a neighbour or your HR at work) with a warning, then consider that as an opportunity to hold yourself back.

If you continue to disregard and avoid listening to all voices from within and outside, then it is an unfortunate situation. You will end up committing a crime and get exposed to punitive action by the law enforcement. Thereafter, it won't be prevention, but only repentance and guilt.

There are five layers of deterrents that prevent you from committing sin. The highest level of minds, lie in the core of the concentric circles. As their ignorance gets clouded and their deterrence moves away from self-awareness to external influence, they move towards the outward layers.

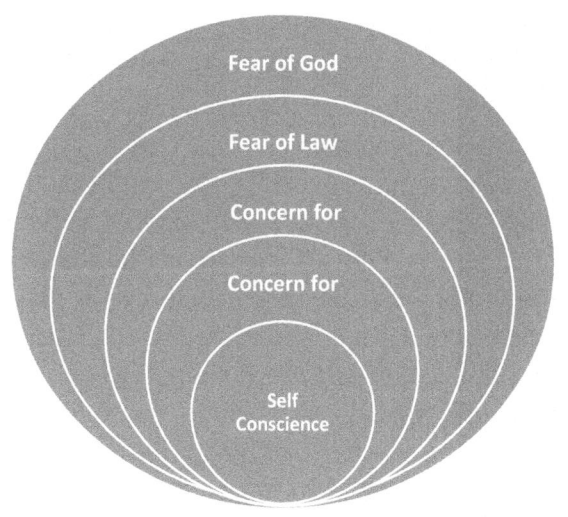

Fear of God
Fear of Law
Concern for
Concern for
Self Conscience

The first is your personal moral code. If you are a person on a high moral ground and listen to your inner voice, then the temptation to sin would not fluster you at all.

The next level is the perceived reaction of your family, friends, and peers. How much do you value their reaction or response to your actions and behaviour? Do you care enough about their expectation from you? You wouldn't walk that path if you care about them.

The third layer is the society at large. Your neighbourhood, the workplace, people distantly related and known to you, the people you interact with often, are the society. They notice you and soon get to know about what you do. Their observation and watching over is a common deterrent for people who care for their own image in the eyes of the society or the community they live in.

The fourth layer is the fear of law. When you know the legal consequences of your action, you would probably think twice before indulging in the act. Most people at the base level of intelligence practice normal behaviour simply for sake of the legal consequences.

The fifth layer is fear of God. There are many simplistic people who have conditioned their minds to recognise several acts as sin. They fear that indulgence in certain actions is sinister and leads to hell. They have a perception about heaven and hell, and with the imagination about hell, no one looks forward to being castigated into it.

Irrespective of which layer of awareness you are into, it is important that there should be some deterrence that applies to you. Anyone lying completely outside this pyramid is incorrigible and is most susceptible to committing a sin.

It is always said that prevention is better than cure. However, if you failed at the stage of prevention and committed a wrong act, you can repent. Realize for once that you were wrong and learn to walk the righteous path. It is important to see the light of wisdom at a point in life and wake up.

There are people who got trapped in a moment and committed a sin. As the moment passed away, they became full of repentance and remorse. There are laws across the world that decide upon some years of punishment for a certain type of crime.

There are directions in scriptures that give hope for absolution from sin if you become aware and start practising self-awareness. Such people who eventually transform, start doing activities for the good of the humanity and in proportions larger than their misdeed. They try to wash their inner muck with splashes of good deeds with the hope to get absolved of their sin.

In addition to Sri Bhagavad Gita, there are other faiths and cultures that hold a similar view about the elements of sin. Here is what a Persian philosopher Al-Ghazali said.

"Declare your jihad on thirteen enemies you cannot see -egoism, arrogance, conceit, selfishness, greed, lust, intolerance, anger, lying, cheating, gossiping and slandering. If you can master and destroy them, then you will be ready to fight the enemy you can see."

He suggests conquering the inner evils first, before tackling with external enemies, and he is so true at that.

Chapter 16: HARNESS THE WANDERING MIND

What is a wandering mind?

The mind is restless, turbulent, obstinate and very strong; the mind is more difficult to control than the wind.

You just came out of the mall with your shopping bags in hand and you could not find your car keys in the right pocket of your trousers where you think you kept it. Instantly, your mind is in a turmoil. Wandering thoughts come to your mind whether you dropped it somewhere in the mall. You drop the shopping bags, pat all your pockets, open your clutch, rummage through all the bags and scatter things desperately. Then you realise the keys are in the inner pocket of your jacket. Peace!!!

A moment ago you were turbulent as a whirlwind and now you are at peace like a calm lake. This is the power of your brain. You faced a situation, and you reacted.

Two cars rubbed against each other on a busy road and their drivers came out for an instant brawl. Road rages have become so commonplace these days.

In some country, a teenager brings a gun to school and opens fire. He injures several and kills someone and probably kills himself too. Do you blame it on the easy gun laws and wish stricter laws?

What would you say about the scorned and dejected youth throwing acid on the face of the girl they apparently loved? Now you want a ban on the sale of acid as well?

An average human gets almost 3000 thoughts per hour or 70000 thoughts per day. This seems like an incessant chatter. The mental conditioning can become such that people have become highly reactive.

Wisdom from The Bhagavad Gita about wandering mind

उद्धरेदात्मनात्मानं नात्मानमवसादयेत् ।
आत्मैव ह्यात्मनो बन्धुरात्मैव रिपुरात्मनः ॥

uddhared-atman-atmanam
natmanam-avasadayet
atmaiva hyatmano bandhur
atmaiva ripur-atmanah

One must conduct oneself with the help of one's mind and not degrade oneself. The mind is the friend of the conditioned soul, and one's enemy as well. –Sri Bhagavad Gita Ch.6; V.5.

बन्धुरात्मात्मात मनस्तस्य येनात्मैवात्मना जितः ।
अनात्मनस्तु शत्रुत्वे वर्तेतात्मैव शत्रुवत् ॥

bandhur-atmat manas-tasya
yen-atmaiva-atmana jitah
anatmastu shatrutve
vartet-atmaiva shatruvat

The mind is the best friend for the one who has conquered it, but the greatest enemy for one who failed at it. –Sri Bhagavad Gita Ch.6; V.6.

यतो यतो निश्चलति मनश्चञ्चलमस्थिरम् ।
ततस्ततो नियम्यैतदात्मन्येव वशं नयेत् ॥

yato yato nishchalati
manascha-chanchalam-sthiram
tatas-tato niyam-yaitad
atmanaiva vansham nayet

Where the mind wanders because of its flickering and unsteady nature, one must withdraw it and bring it back under self control. −Sri Bhagavad Gita Ch.6; V.26.

श्रीभगवानुवाच
असंशयं महाबाहो मनो दुर्निग्रहं चलम् ।
अभ्यासेन तु कौन्तेय वैराग्येण च गृह्यते ॥

shri-bhagavan-uvacha
asamshayam mahabaho
mano durnigraham chalam
abhyasen tu kaunteya
vairagyen cha griha-yate

Lord Sri Krishna said: O mighty-armed son of Kunti. It is undoubtedly very difficult to curb the restless mind, but it still is possible by suitable practice and by detachment. −Sri Bhagavad Gita Ch.6; V.35.

Learning from the scriptures

The mind causes bondage and liberation. If one has submitted himself / herself to one's senses and conducts his/ her life unmindfully, then it is a bondage. For the conscious people, who harness their senses and control them, can experience liberation.

When your mind acts against you, and you have no control over it, then you hardly need an external enemy to destroy you. Your own uncontrolled wandering mind shall become your greatest enemy.

The nature of the mind is flickering and unsteady. If you cup your palms around the flickering candle flame, you make it steady. Likewise, if you control the external influences, you can control the steadiness of the mind.

Detachment from wrongful actions is the first step towards controlling the restless, wandering mind. Difficult as it may sound, but with practice and persistence it is attainable.

How to control a wandering mind?
1.   **Meditation** - When I initially asked people about meditation, I was told that to meditate, one must sit in a peaceful seclusion and zero your thoughts into the steady flame of a candle or a dot on the wall. Reduce the flow of your thoughts and freeze them into nothingness.

Spiritual mystic Sadguru Jaggi says, *"It is the conspiracy of the stupid against human intelligence, suggesting that, to meditate is to freeze the brain."*

It took billions of years of evolution for the humans for their minds to think in a way they do now. Do you really want to stop and freeze your brain?

So how do we prevent our brain from wandering? When you eat a wrong food, the body responds with a diarrhoea. Likewise, when the mind consumes wrong data or wrong inputs, one ends up with a mental diarrhoea and the uncontrolled mind reacts crazily.

The human mind is a powerful tool, so use it wisely and rightly. Ensure that your mind stops consuming wrong thoughts. Filter your thoughts with wisdom and exercise discretion between right and wrong.

2. **Distancing** - I was driving through the city and got stuck in the traffic several times. I felt helpless because I could do nothing about the dense traffic. Several thoughts were rambling in my mind. I was driving with family to a hill station, so I wanted to steer clear soon. Gradually I left the traffic behind and found an empty road. As I drove up the hills, I could see the valley shrinking down below me. They were stuck in traffic, but I was soaring. A while ago I was amid that conundrum, and as soon as I rose above them, they appeared so insignificant and small. Once you elevate your thinking to a certain level, you will distance yourself from the chatter. A higher level of consciousness can help a person stay aloof from the useless chatter of this immensely powerful thinking machine and rein in the thoughts and sensory experiences that are like unbridled horses. A controlled mind is a powerful tool that can get used for performing complex tasks at your command.

3. **Live in the moment** - The uncontrolled mind wastes plenty of energy and efforts in re-processing the experiences and imagining the unseen future. One wastes a significant part of one's life in brooding and lamenting about what got lost in the past. Another type of people remains under constant fear and anxiety about the future. This prevents one to live in the present moment and as a result one cannot cherish the life as it moves on. To prevent the mind from wandering, please focus on now and live in the moment. There are things far more in our control than we imagine. We can do a lot about the

present moment if we look into the problems that are at hand.

4. **Use distractions** - Use a deliberate distraction to silence the unwanted noises in the mind. Music is a great remedy and a healer for the hurt mind. Chanting of mantras is a powerful remedy to focus the mind. A robust exercise or physical activity can also help to distract the mental conundrum. A friend of mine is a musician who has also written books. I asked him what does he do for calming his mind. Read a book or listen to music? He said he is a musician first, so if he listens to music, his mind forces him to analyse the notes of the guitarist or the beats of the drummer. So he finds recluse in reading books instead. Likewise, a literary person would overthink while reading a book so he/she might find solace in listening to music. Discover your own zone that helps you to distract yourself from overbearing thoughts. This distraction actually becomes your point of focus and helps to harness the wandering mind.

5. **Use calming techniques** - Using an oil burner with lavender oil, sipping green tea with chamomile, putting away electronic gadgets, taking a warm bath, or taking a nap may help you calm down. Discover any activity that helps you calm the mind. Lighting up a cigarette or gulping a few shots of alcohol might seem like an easy hack initially, but they are addictive and habit forming besides being harmful. Sometimes just sitting by yourself and doing nothing is also a great way (and my most favourite way) to calmness.

The monkey mind

Once a traveller was walking through a lonely place. He was sweating and was tired. When he came across a gentle stream flowing by, he stopped for a while, and drank some cool water from it. Then he felt the indulgence to take a plunge. So he took off his shoes and clothes to waddle through the stream. He took a dip and as his head emerged above the sheaths of water, he was terrified to see that a monkey carried off his back-pack and sat atop a tree.

That bag had all his belongings and he needed it back desperately. He ran helter skelter shouting for help but there was no one in sight. Then he found a small hut. He tapped the door and pleaded for help. An old man came out and heard his plight. He went inside and returned with two bananas. He accompanied the traveller upto that tree and they saw that the monkey was biting and ripping the bag.

The old man hurled a banana at the monkey. The monkey held the bag in one hand and caught the banana with the other. Then the man threw another banana at him. The monkey couldn't resist the banana so he dropped the bag and caught the banana. The traveller got back his bag and thanked the old man profusely.

In most cultures, a wandering mind is equated with a monkey. How to control this monkey? Just as the monkey had to let go of the loot to hold the bananas. We have to give our minds some higher, deeper, and more meaningful experiences which gives greater pleasure our mind elsewhere to let go of the mental garbage.

If we learn to connect with our spiritual self, we can learn to connect with our true nature and through that, attain inner peace.

On a lighter note, a South Africa author Mokokoma Mokhonoana said, *"The mind is a sweetheart, when it is wondering; and a bitch, when it is wandering."*

Chapter 17: THE VIRTUE OF FORGIVENESS

What is Forgiveness?

In my book The Secrets To A Magical Life, I have dealt with this topic at length. However, for sake of brevity I shall repurpose some content here to bring the subject into the context.

When there is insolent hurt, it fills you inside with negativity. This needs venting either by inconsolable crying or revenge. Recuperation from the persistent horrible pressure about a profound and chaotic injury is like one that continues mending over, yet with soil, garbage, everything caught inside. Mending is not a direct procedure; you continue tearing the injury open, or not, and the deeper you uncover to clear the garbage, the closer you get to being all right. It feels like a splinter of injury tucked some place too deep inside to even think about reaching.

Forgiving is not about shaking hands or hugging your tormentor or praying for him. It is about just you and your profundity. It is you who need the healing. Pull the splinter out from your heart and give yourself a chance to heal. You may live and move on without bearing the cross of guilt for having got hurt. Do not stoop low to retaliate with violence. The muck should clear from your heart first. Once you attain the absolution, the fire of revenge shall subside and will change your perspective.

Wisdom from The Bhagavad Gita about forgiveness

तस्मात्प्रणम्य प्रणिधाय कायं
प्रसादये त्वामहमीशमीड्यम् ।

पतिव पुत्रस्य सखेव सख्युः
पुरयिः पुरयियार्हसि देव सोढुम् ॥

*tasmaat-pranamya pranidhaaya kaayam
prasaadaye tvaam-aham-isham-idyam
piteva putrasya sakhev sakhyuh
priyah priyayaharsi dev sodhum*

I fall down to offer You my respectful obeisance and seek Your mercy, O Supreme Lord, worshiped by every living being. Forgive me for my wrong doings just as a father forgives the impudence of his son, a friend the impertinence of a friend, or a husband the mistakes of his wife. –Sri Bhagavad Gita Ch.11; V.44.

Learning from the scriptures

Seeking forgiveness is the first step towards realising imperfection of self. Such humility makes space for the person to absolve himself/herself from vexation.

Introspective and humble people attain self-awareness because they are of equipoise in happiness and distress.

Forgiveness is one of the few transcendental qualities bestowed upon people with divine nature.

How to practice forgiveness?

<u>Forgive yourself first</u>

A person, who is a self-critique, finds it very hard to forgive one-self. Such persons are unforgiving. They cannot forgive themselves as much as they cannot forgive others, and they constrain their quality of mercy.

Life becomes miserable when a person cannot move on from the past standpoint. The burden weighs upon his/her chest and suffocates him/her for life. From this stubbornness emerges self-pity, which is a bigger evil. Sometimes they got wronged or abused in their childhood, and they bear the cross of guilt for the sins of another. They blame themselves and pity themselves and cannot lead a pleasant quality of life.

Remove your resentment, blame and shame. It is difficult. It requires a firm resolve and willingness to undo the guilt. Try to reason in your own defence. You were not the controller of all circumstances.

Sit relaxed, close your eyes and look inward. Let your active consciousness look into yourself. Seek forgiveness from self. Admit you meant no harm but are apologetic too. Resolve that you want to cleanse yourself of the guilt and move on.

Forgive yourself. Let it go. If you still cannot move on from it, please seek professional help before the manifestations become profound. Suicidal tendencies can happen if this guilt doesn't get taken care of.

"If I hadn't forgiven myself, I wouldn't be strong enough to love someone this much."– Dawn Lanuza, The Hometown Hazard

Seek Forgiveness

It takes a strong heart to realise that one has wronged someone and there is a need to beg pardon for that. Our selfishness and ego makes us sin, lie, cheat, steal, hurt, mistreat and the negative karma shall follow us and tarnish our soul forever. Even the craftiest sinner would know in his own heart about his own wrongdoing.

How to ask forgiveness? First realise within yourself that you were wrong. Resolve that your wrong action will not recur. Humble yourself and begin with a sincere apology to the person you have wronged.

Do not add excuses and stories to justify your wrong action. If you are justifying, then perhaps you are not sorry. Do not plan to get away cheap by just uttering the word sorry without meaning it from the heart.

Be prepared to accept how the person reacts towards your apology. The person might not approve of your actions but might forgive you to move on. It is also possible that they do not condition their conscience to forgiveness.

If they forgive, their burden shall be light and your burden too will lighten with the thought nobody is cursing you anymore. If they cannot forgive, they will carry the burden as much as you do.

Still, if you have apologised, there would be chances for you to feel lighter because you have realised within and sought forgiveness.

"I have learned that sometimes 'sorry' is not enough. Sometimes you actually have to change." – Claire London

Erase a past hurt

Sometimes we feel hurt or wronged. It could be through someone very near or close to us. It could be mere harsh words of admonition, or the guilt of a student who failed in board exams, or a couple that abused and ruined their marriage; an event that occupied some vital space inside you like a thorn in the flesh. You could not overcome that hurt. You still get a lump in your throat if you just think about it. What do you do?

NLP or Neuro Linguistic Programming is a practice that helps you erase the memory of your past hurt and then re-wire your brain to be futuristic.

This is how you do it. Sit and close your eyes. Recall that incidence. Imagine you can see that event being projected on a wall in front of you.

Imagine that action replaying in all its colours and sound. Now imagine that you've shut off the sound.

What you now see is a silent movie. Gradually, eliminate the action.

What you now see is a still picture. Now, remove all the colours.

You now see a black and white frozen image, as fragile as a drawing made with white chalk on a blackboard.

Now hold something in your hand as if you are holding a duster and swing your hand to wipe off that blackboard.

Do that once, and if need arises, repeat after sometime. You will feel relieved as the noises in your head get erased. This is a proven technique to erase hurtful memories from the sub-conscious layers of your mind.

After erasing negativity, rewire and reprogram yourself with positivity. So close your eyes again and play along with some soft meditative music. Imagine yourself walking down the path of life. Imagine how you set the next milestone and how you reach there. Imagine how you solve your perceived problems. Imagine your dear ones acknowledging you for your achievements.

Set goals. Set milestones. Make that imagination, your blueprint for the future. Keep inspiring yourself by repeating this exercise.

It is not self-hypnosis because you need a lot of expertise for hypnotism. It is more about dealing with the sub-conscious layer of your mind in an easier manner.

"All that we are results from what we have thought. The mind is everything. What we think we become." - The Buddha.

Forgive Others

Human conscience has plenty of errors and lack of perfection. We must learn to give a second chance. Forgive others, as we wish to seek forgiveness for ourselves.

To forgive someone is not to endorse the wrong doer or feed his / her ego by absolving their sin. Forgiveness is the art of moving on from the resentment to enlighten one's own heart and not bear the burden of guilt and anger.

To forgive others is to tell oneself that I am entitled to a better life with no burden on my heart. I am done with this situation and from now I distance myself from it. I am washed and absolved and renewed into a new life. This resolution from within helps you get rid of your excess baggage that you do not carry henceforth.

"Forgiveness is not always easy. At times, it feels more painful than the wound we suffered, to forgive the one that inflicted it. And yet, there is no peace without forgiveness." – Marianne Williamson

Chapter 18: SEEKING PEACE

What is Peace?

Shalom! This is a greeting in many regions of this world, which means "may peace be with you!" It is commonplace to wish and greet someone with a blessing for something that is scarce. In the war-torn trouble ridden zones, peace is the rarest commodity. Hence the greeting.

When I started my journey to study the philosophy of life, I read many works which suggested that peace is the ultimate pursuit of life. This myth got shattered when I read the Bhagavad Gita, which clearly stated that peace is the foundation and pre-requisite for any happiness and pursuit in life.

Without being peaceful, one cannot even enjoy a meal or hum a song by oneself.

There are two levels of peace.
1. Internal peace
2. External peace

Internal peace or inner peace is the peace of your mind and soul. It is a state of calm, serenity and tranquility of mind. We cannot have peace with others unless we are at peace with ourselves.

External peace is built on the foundation of inner peace. It is being at peace with others around us at the social level, national level and world level.

Wisdom from The Bhagavad Gita about peace

नास्ति बुद्धिरयुक्तस्य न चायुक्तस्य भावना ।
न चाभावयतः शान्तिरशान्तस्य कुतः सुखम् ॥

*naasti buddhir-ayuktasya
na chayuktasya bhaavna
na chabhavyatah shantir
ashantasya krutah sukham*

One who is not connected with the Supreme can have neither transcendental intelligence nor a steady mind, without which there is no avail of peace. How can there be any happiness without peace? –Sri Bhagavad Gita Ch.2; V.66.

विहाय कामान्यः सर्वान्पुमांश्चरति निःस्पृहः ।
निर्ममो निरहङ्कार स शान्तिमधिगच्छति ॥

*vihāya kāmān yaḥ sarvān

pumāṁś carati niḥspṛhaḥ

nirmamo nirahaṅkāraḥ
sa śāntim adhigacchati*

A person who has given up all desires for sense gratification, who lives free from desires, who has given up all sense of proprietorship and is devoid of false ego; he alone can attain real peace. - Sri Bhagavad Gita Ch.2; V.71.

श्रद्धावाँल्लभते ज्ञानं तत्परः संयतेन्द्रियः ।
ज्ञानं लब्ध्वा परां शान्तिमचिरेणाधिगच्छति ॥

*shraddhavan-labhate gyanam
tatparah sanyatendriyah
gyanam labdhva paraam
shantim-chirenadhi-gachhati*

A faithful man who is dedicated to transcendental knowledge and who subdues his senses is eligible to achieve such knowledge, and having achieved it he quickly attains the supreme spiritual peace. –Sri Bhagavad Gita Ch.4; V.39.

भोक्तारं यज्ञतपसां सर्वलोकमहेश्वरम् ।
सुहृदं सर्वभूतानां ज्ञात्वा मां शान्तमृच्छति ॥

bhoktaram yagya-tapasaam
sarva-loka-maheshwaram
su-hridam sarva-bhutanam
gyatva maam shantim-richhati

A person in full consciousness of Me, knowing Me to be the ultimate beneficiary of all sacrifices and austerities, the Supreme Lord of all planets and demigods, and the benefactor and well-wisher of all living beings, attains peace from the pangs of material miseries. –Sri Bhagavad Gita Ch.5; V.29.

Learning from the scriptures

Peace is not a goal, but a pre-requisite for happiness. There can be no peace without self-awareness.

To attain real peace, one has to give up gratification of sensory pleasures. Unfulfilled desires make one restless.

Peace lies in pursuit of self-awareness through transcendental knowledge.

The eightfold *yoga* mysticism gets automatically practiced in Krishna consciousness because it serves the ultimate purpose. There is a gradual process of elevation in the practice of *yama, niyama, asana, pranayama, pratyahara, dharana, dhyana and Samadhi.*

One who gains philosophical knowledge under the guidance of a spiritual master and practices many austerities and penances attains eternal peace and happiness.

How to seek Peace?

Peace is a calm state of mind. It is a state of mind where there will be a gentle flow of thoughts but no thoughts are bothering. The mind acts like the surface of water. Drop a gravel in it and there will be turbulent ripples. Likewise, at the slightest provocation, the mind reacts with resistance and turbulence. There are two ways to look at the concentric waves on the surface of water. (1) It is a turbulence or disturbance (2) It is the pattern of fluidity so accept it and make sense out of it.

1. **Accept yourself** - Our acceptability for the outside world stems from how much we accept ourselves. A part of our resentment comes from the way we compare our ineptness with people we admire. We always wish we could be like them. We can become a bit like them if we try real hard, but we shall become an inferior copy. Why be a poor copy of someone else when you could be better off just being yourself? Nobody is perfect and everyone makes mistakes. Be kind and forgiving, specially forgiving yourself for the person who you think you should be but couldn't be. Do your own maximum to the best of your own ability. Just aim to become the best version of yourself.

2. **Live in this moment** - There are researches claiming that the mind generates 60-70 thousand thoughts per day. What are these thoughts? Those are reflections from the memory or imaginations of expectations about the future. There is a constant tug of war between these two kinds of thoughts. The experiences could bug one, unable to move on from them. Or one could be anxious about the future and its uncertainties. We often build future anticipation around experiences. If the past was a wonderful experience, a person would have rosy expectations about a dreamy future, mixed by an insecurity of dreams realising as per expectation. However, if the experiences were not good, then the expectations from the future can be even worse and the imagination of it could be horrifying. Both the past and future thoughts can ruin a perfect present. Besides the present tense of time, the word present also means a 'gift'. This present moment that we live in is a perfect gift, only if we can unwrap it. Everyone gets the same quantum of time each day, but everyone uses their time differently. The winner is the one who spends his/her time happily. Find happiness in everything you do. Do whatever that makes you happy. Those who can live into the present moment and find happiness in it are more peaceful within than those who cannot.

3. **Spreading happiness** - One cannot truly enjoy happiness all by self without creating an ambience of happiness around oneself. Begin with your family. The first thing you need to provide for your family is love. The basic purpose of creating a family is to share love. Always remember to prioritise love over anything else. Sharing food, comforts, and space with the family comes after the primary need for sharing love. As you spread the ambience further, you are a part of your workplace and your society around you. Check if your

presence makes people happy. People will be happy with you if you are helpful and dependable. Try to help people as much as you can. Good karma returns, and so does bad. Let people feel the confidence that you are a person they can depend upon for help when required. The reciprocation of your love and help will enable peace to prevail upon you naturally.

Peace decoded

Peace is not being in a place where there is no noise, trouble, hardwork or difficulty. It is about being in the middle of all mayhem and chaos and yet stay calm and focussed to make the inward journey. Spirituality brings the inner calm and peace amidst all difficulties surrounding us.

In the Buddhist scripture Dhammapada, there are some pointers to inner peace. They are:

- **Attachment leads to suffering**- The material possessions we hold on to will wither away, the people we love shall part some day. Holding on to your attachment deep-rootedly will cause suffering. Hence let go of your obsessive attachment first.
- **Desiring the right things** – To crave for deep desires is wrong but there is nothing wrong to desire for good things. Focus on the good things in life for self and others.
- **Persuing sensual pleasures are source of suffering** – Sensual pleasures pertain to lust. However, use your senses for constructive purposes and not as an irresponsible pleasure seeker.
- **From misery grows beauty** – The seed breaks and a plant grows. A diamond is cut and scrubbed for it to shine. Buddha experienced misery that led to his enlightenment. So do not get flustered with misery. There can be a rewarding outcome after your hardships.

- **Good company is important** – A bad company will bring bad influences while good company will create a positive environment.
- **A trained mind leads to happiness** – Buddhism has a lot of emphasis on meditation and mindfulness. Like how a body can be trained to build strong muscles, the mind can be trained to perform immense tasks.
- **Short term evil will have long term consequences** – Refrain from indulging in any wrong activity because no matter how small, it shall have long term consequences.

"Never be in a hurry; do everything quietly and in a calm spirit. Do not lose your inner peace for anything what-so-ever, even if your entire world seems upset." —Saint Francis de Sales.

Chapter 19: DEVELOP SELF AWARENESS – THE CONCLUSION

His Holiness Adi Sankaracharya was an Indian philosopher and theologian who merged the doctrine of Advaita Vedanta. His works elaborate on ideas found in the Upanishads. He also explained the key difference between Hinduism and Buddhism, stating that Hinduism asserts "Atman (Soul, Self) exists", while Buddhism asserts that there is no Soul, no Self." [Wiki]

Adi Sankara said that it is rare to be born as a human and it is even rarer to have steadfastness on the spiritual path. For this, it is pertinent to have a correct understanding of the scriptures. He added that three things can happen only by the grace of God.

1. Birth as a human
2. A burning desire for liberation
3. Receiving guidance from an enlightened guru

The first step to liberation is complete dis-association from things that are impermanent. When you begin a project to clean the river, the first thing you need to do it to stop ejecting effluents and sewage into it. Avoid the objects of sensory pleasures because they hinder the process of enlightenment.

Then the next step is to follow calmness, self-control, forbearance, and complete renunciation of selfish actions and cultivate the virtues of contentment, compassion, forgiveness, straight-forwardness, calmness, and self-control.

To attain enlightenment, we must first understand what we are composed of. The absolute human entity comprises five sheaths. We have these five subtle layers corresponding to the five elements of our inner structure. i.e. (Earth, Water, Fire, Air and Space)

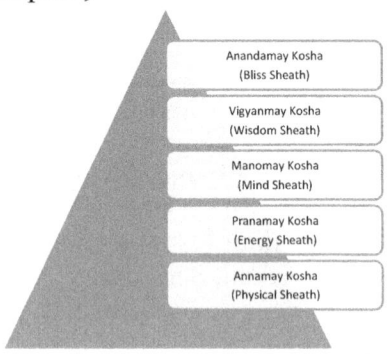

Anandamay Kosha (Bliss Sheath)
Vigyanmay Kosha (Wisdom Sheath)
Manomay Kosha (Mind Sheath)
Pranamay Kosha (Energy Sheath)
Annamay Kosha (Physical Sheath)

Let us study this pyramid from the bottom to top.

1. **Annamay Kosha** (earth element) or the physical sheath or the food sheath is the physical body that comprises the food that we consume. We are what we eat. It formed the zygote with the fusion of two microscopic cells. Thereafter it accumulates nutrition, first through the mother's umbilical cords, then through her breast milk and thereafter by consuming food from external sources. We have a unique system that converts every morsel of food into a part of us. We identify this layer the most because it is in absolute physical form and we have the sensory organs to gather our experiences from it.

We can strengthen this layer by regulating our food and diet. Eat what is right for you and in the right manner.

2. **Pranamay Kosha** (water element) or the energy sheath is the life and respirational activity at the cellular level and the organic level. Water forms the vital fluids not only as blood and electrolytes but also maintains life at the cellular level. Vital energy flows through the body cells as we breathe. A lot of sub-conscious involuntary actions get performed by the body unmindfully.

We can re-vitalise our body through the water we drink. Consume clean drinking water mindfully as if you are consuming the source of life. 60% of our body is water.

3. **Manomay Kosha** (fire element) is the mind sheath. This is the level of conscious mind and emotions. The mind can think and direct the body into action. It permeates through the food and vitality sheaths. We experience the energy flow through our emotions and realize our thoughts and judgement.

We fueled the fire in our body with the air we breathe. Practice mindful breathing. Pranayama is one element of yoga with which we can enhance our overall well-being.

4. **Vigyanamay Kosha** (air element) is the Wisdom sheath. It is the power of discretion, our inner knowledge and wisdom. The thoughts have to be processed in a mindful manner to make sense of our life. Our thoughts control our actions, which bear the consequences. Our thoughts can travel faster than the wind and with as much force as well. We can converge this enormous force into one focus to perform tasks that are un-imaginable by most people.

To harness the power of our thoughts into a tool to perform special tasks, we have to meditate. Meditation alone can channelize your thoughts in the desired direction.

5. **Anandamay Kosha** (space element) is the bliss sheath. It is the experience of inner peace and joy which is free from our thoughts, emotions, energy, vitality and body, yet it embraces them all. Experiencing this layer of you requires proper understanding and sensitivity. Once you train yourself to understand this layer of your existence, you will feel there is an inner spring which wells out joyfulness from within with no external stimulation.

To enhance this faculty of ours, we need the guidance of a spiritual master or guru who can help us identify our inner self.

H.H. Adi Sankara has emphasized upon how one can distinguish between Self (Real) and Ignorance (Unreal) and direct one's self-awareness towards becoming an enlightened being.

Swami Paramahansa Yogananda was an Indian Hindu monk, yogi and guru who had introduced millions to the teachings of meditation and Kriya Yoga through his organization Self-Realization Fellowship (SRF) / Yogoda Satsanga Society (YSS) of India, during the late 19th and early 20th centuries. He was chief disciple of the yoga guru Swami Sri Yukteswar Giri. His lineage sent him to spread the teachings of yoga to the West, to prove the unity between Eastern and Western religions and to preach a balance between Western material growth and Indian spirituality. He lived his last 32 years in America. His long-standing influence in the American yoga movement, and especially the yoga culture of Los Angeles, led him to be considered by yoga experts as the "Father of Yoga in the West." Swami Yogananda gave a general description of Kriya Yoga in his *Autobiography*:

"The Kriya Yogi mentally directs his life energy to revolve, upward and downward, around the six spinal centres (medullary, cervical, dorsal, lumbar, sacral, and coccygeal plexuses) which correspond to the twelve astral signs of the zodiac, the symbolic Cosmic Man. One-half-minute of revolution of energy around the sensitive spinal cord of man effects subtle progress in his evolution; that half-minute of Kriya equals one year of natural spiritual unfoldment." [Wiki]

Swami Paramhansa Yogananda shared a beautiful example of difference between material and spiritual pursuits. We see people chase wealth and other material pursuits; they put in enormous hard work, yet wealth is elusive. This causes unhappiness and resentment. Whereas those in spiritual pursuit appear to be happier despite fewer material achievements. Hence material achievements can satisfy only your physical needs. Your spiritual side needs spiritual advancement in life. There is a distinct energy that fuels the soul. Yet, how does one tell whether one is on the right spiritual path?

Spiritual pursuit is like sowing a seed. You do not take the seed out of soil to check if it has germinated. That would only hamper the growth. So, with the seeds of spiritual efforts, you just have to plant them, leave them there, and tend to them carefully, nurture them with conscious practices of meditation and reasoning.

The nature runs its show with a minimal effort. There are unimaginable miraculous wonders happening in the nature yet they seem to happen so effortlessly. Forests grow without requiring us human to sow the seeds and water them. River flows, requiring no one to pump the water. Various life forms in millions of numbers thrive, requiring no one to feed them. The Sun rises and sets every day with a certain precision. The seasons run a relay race, passing the batons flawlessly. The nature gives bountiful gifts to us all, yet we receive unmindful of the giver and provider of all resources.

Material pursuits require constant efforts, yet success is not in proportion to the efforts. All efforts can go in vain. However, in the spiritual path, your efforts do not get wasted. You have sown the seed and it shall grow. You just have to nurture it enough. A whole-hearted seeker is never unsuccessful. Perseverance and unrelenting enthusiasm leads to the magical path to success.

Swami Abhedananda was a direct disciple of the mystic Sri Ramakrishna Paramhansa in the 19th Century. He formally became a sannyasi along with Swami Vivekananda and others and was a well known Advaita Vedanta philosopher. He travelled extensively across London, New York, Canada, Mexico, Japan, Hong Kong and travelled on foot across the Himalayas to reach Tibet. He formed the Ramakrishna Vedanta Society in Kolkata in 1923. [Wiki]

He said that our mind goes through five stages before enlightenment.
1. Moodha
2. Kshipta
3. Vikshipta
4. Ekagrah
5. Niruddha

MOODHA is the stupid or confused. In this state, the mind is dull, lazy, inactive, idiotic. It envelops the intellect and understanding in the darkness of ignorance.

KSHIPTA is the scattered state. In this state, the mind is hyperactive, restless, directionless, wanders aimlessly, uncontrollably and engage in purposeless activities. In this state, a person has a firm belief in self-righteousness. They feel insecure if checked by another person.

VIKSHIPTA is the state of oscillation or alternately active or dull. The mind becomes active and reverts to the dull state when confused.

We find the above three states of mind in ordinary people, and it doesn't help them attain spirituality. Of these, the first two are the extreme states of hyper active and inactive mind.

EKAGRAH is focussed mind. This is the ability of the mind to stay focussed and follow one direction. In this state, the mind can concentrate. A person who can focus and concentrate can transcend to higher levels of spiritual awareness. Thus, a calm and peaceful mind is a pre-requisite and the beginning of your spiritual journey.

NIRUDDHA is well controlled concentration in which all involuntary activities are subdued and controlled by the sub conscious mind. The mind transcends from the limited ordinary capacity to the extra-ordinary and super-conscious state of self-awareness.

Is Meditation the key to all problems?

The modern world often defines meditation as a process whereas it is consequence if certain process is followed. Meditativeness is a state of mind you would love to be in. It is not a moment of transcendence that you would like to visit sometimes but would like to remain in it all the time.

For this, you have to obliterate the boundaries of your external identity and cultivate your body, mind and energy to a certain level so that you may reach the meditative state.

To cultivate your body, mind and energies you have to adopt the yogic lifestyle which is inclusive of all the factors, like sleep, yoga, diet, water, breathing and mindfulness. You need to attain a state of peace and forgiveness to contition your mind for performing higher level of tasks.

Hence, let this be clear that meditation is not the process but the goal. It is not the activity to begin with but the state of mind to reach at a certain goal.

The process of self-awareness

The process of self-awareness and awakening requires three major practices in life.
1. The power of Reasoning
2. The power of Intuition
3. The power of Restraint

Power of Reasoning

The power of reasoning uses perceptions, conceptualisation and sensitivity. One can, with some practice, develop the power of reasoning.

When thoughts appear in your mind, analyse with reasoning, ask why, drill down why after why until you arrive at the root cause. Usually you would arrive at the root cause within four to five iterations of 'why'. Does it sound convincing? Initially, it made sense to me, because as a black belt in Six Sigma, I have studied about the 5 why technique and root cause analysis and I could easily relate to it. This was until I heard a counter view.

Dr. Tasha Eurich, an entrepreneur, pairing her human behavioural science with a practical approach to solving business challenges, has helped leaders improve their effectiveness. In her discourse at a TEDx talk, she brought out some interesting facts. To her, self-awareness is the ability to see ourselves clearly, to understand who we are, how others see us and how we set ourselves against this world. It empowers us to see ourselves. We might not like what we see but get more comfort in knowing ourselves. Self-aware people are more fulfilled, stronger in relationships, more creative, confident, communicative, less likely to lie, cheat and steal. They perform better at work and are more promotable and are more effective leaders.

Surprisingly, 95% of us believe we are self-aware, but only 10 to 15% actually are. Introspection is important, but research shows that those who were too introspective and asked why were more stressed and depressed with themselves. Asking why is like looking into the rear-view mirror while driving. That would surely lead to crashing against a light post. When we ask why, we often start inventing answers which we think are right while they actually aren't. This doesn't mean that we stop introspecting, but we must do it in the right way. So how should we introspect?

To start, we just need to change one simple word. Instead of **'why'** just ask **'what'**. The 'why' question is looking backwards through the rear-view mirror, while the what questions are looking forward to some positive action.

It makes a big difference when instead of asking "why I am unsuccessful?" you ask "what are the ingredients to success? What can I do to become more successful?"

Power of Intuition

Katrine Kjaer is a dynamic e-commerce professional. She is the Managing Director of Valmano, a German online store for watches and jewellery. Katrine has a unique combination of creative thinking and technical knowledge. In one of her TEDx talks, she said, while interviewing candidates to hire them, we find their CV is great and when asked, they come across with smart and intelligent answers that you cannot logically deny. It takes a lot of intuitiveness to cut through the layers deep enough to check the level of trust and connection with the team.

The power of intuition usually remains undeveloped because of lack of guidance & training. Develop the habit of finding the truth in everything and develop immediate comprehension of truth. Learn step-by-step method of yoga and deep meditation that leads to self realisation, because meditation is the way.

Intuition manifests in the calm consciousness. Usually this feeling comes from within, however, when it comes in meditation, it comes through a definite sense of right direction and unshakable conviction.

Sadguru Jaggi Vasudev says intuition is not just another dimension of perception, but it is computing. It is just that you don't take all the logical steps but make a leap to arrive at a decision. Looking at the sky, a farmer can tell when it is going to rain, much before the meteorologist can pronounce the possibility of its occurrence with the help of scientific instruments.

However, intuitive decisions get looked up to with trust and respect because it bypasses logical research. When one has to succeed beyond a certain point, there are some things where one has jumped those steps arrive at an intuitive decision. It is just that you don't have to walk through that many steps and pass through the maze of logical reasoning. Else, you will end up freaking out with every minor aspect in life.

Intuition is definitely a more successful way to conduct your life. It is certainly not a guesswork. To develop intuition, learn how to sit with full alertness, yet not thinking about anything. Do you find that impossible? Learn that the difference lies in paying 'attention'. The most important aspect is your '**attention**' and not your '**thoughts**'. This one change alone can make you more intuitive.

How do you deal with your distractions? Regardless of whether you decided through intuition or logical reasoning, people would protest if that doesn't fall in line with their expectations. Hence, there isn't much you can do about things that are beyond you.

In the yogic system, the significance of intuition is as important as the logic. Living a balanced life helps deal with complex situations with ease, only when the intuition of your mind is sufficiently evolved and developed. When you become intuitive, you will hear the voices from the heaven.

Meditation is the only way to discriminate between truth and fallacy. Intuition bridges the chasm between intellectual knowledge of the soul and actual realisation of the divine self. The divine knowledge speaks through your inner voice. It is a feeble voice, and you must develop the art of silence and introspection to look inwards. When you do not listen to your inner voice, it becomes silent.

Power of Restraint

Mr. Ishwar C Puri was the Chief Secretary of Punjab during his stint in the 60s, but he was an enlightened person. He once described how some teachers have visualised the detachment of five vices of the mind (lust, anger, ego, greed, possessiveness).

He laughed at the funny description that it is akin to a crow that plunges into a lake of serenity and emerges out of it as a swan and the five vices (kaama, krodha, madha, lobha, moha) turn into five small boys and walk away. In reality, that never happens. These vices are not entirely your enemies but tools for you to use. They are instrumental in performance of karma. It is hard to tell when and how much one uses these tools in performance of karma, and how much turns into a sinister activity.

However, in the path of spiritualism, these vices become impediments and with the right type of meditation, these vices fall off like dead leaves. There isn't any dramatic action that causes these vices to walk away from you, but you need to practice a lot of restraint, which is possible through meditation.

What happens when someone hurts you unnecessarily? How do you react to a provocation? When you react instantly and jump into action, you create a new karma. When you let it go, you end the cycle of karma. You must have heard that count up to ten before you react with anger. Indeed, that helps. A delayed reaction helps to practice restraint. Instant reaction flares up negative karma, whereas a calm composure wards off unnecessary karma.

I hope to impress upon my readers that the powers of reasoning, intuition and restraint when rightly put into practice, help us awaken to our self-awareness.

Is there a God?

There is not a community in this world that isn't gripped by their own religious beliefs. Their beliefs have kept them united, although it has divided the human-kind. Also there are atheists and rationalists who spend all their lives to convince people that there is no God.

The knowledge about whether there is a God or no God are both useless information. Would there be a good reason to behave better if there is God because of the fear of being observed and judged by someone above? Also you have always yearned to reach heaven someday and were always petrified with the thoughts of landing into hell. Would there be a different and irresponsible behaviour if there is no God?

Instead of seeking to know whether there is God or no God, it is better to seek inside oneself to realise the inner being. Do you realise who you are? How do you choose to live your life?

You can spend the whole life believing there is God and that would be driven by fear more than love, or you could spend your life in thinking there is no God and behave in a self-centric manner only to resent later.

What you can surely do without having to regret later is to realise yourself and be awakened to self-awareness so that you can live a meaningful and purposeful life.

At the end of your life, if you are satisfied, calm, peaceful, free from any guilt or regret, then you know that you have lived your life well.

Living the Life as is...

Life is a simple phenomenon, but it can get as complex as you make it. One can handle life with much ease, if one decides to live the life as it is. I came across a lovely poem by Lee Tzu Pheng (Singapore Cultural Medallion Winner) which speaks a lot about the type of attitude one should have towards life.

I conclude my story, hoping these lines would linger on in your thoughts for a long time. While reading this poem, I sometimes substitute the words 'Sip your Tea' with 'Live your Life' and the fun begins.

Sip your Tea
Nice and Slow,

No one Ever knows
when it's Time to Go,
There'll be no Time
to enjoy the Glow,
So sip your Tea
Nice and Slow...

Life is too Short but
feels pretty Long,
There's too Much to do, so much going Wrong,
And Most of the Time You Struggle to be Strong,
Before it's too Late
and it's time to Go,
Sip your Tea
Nice and Slow...

Some Friends stay,

others Go away,
Loved ones are Cherished, but not all will Stay,
Kids will Grow up, and Fly away,
There's really no saying how things will Go,
So sip your Tea
Nice and Slow...

In the End it's really
all about Understanding Love,
For this World
and in the Stars above,
Appreciate and Value who truly Cares,
Smile and Breathe
and let your Worries go,
So, Just Sip your Tea
Nice and Slow....

ONE MOMENT PLEASE

I thank you with deep gratitude for having read this book till the end. You could have read any other book, but you chose this one and I sincerely hope this was worth your time.

I hope you found practical solutions to your questions about problems in life, and if you liked my work, I request you to please spend a few moments to follow through this link and post a feedback on Amazon. Please click here.

If you have any suggestions or questions about this book, you can reach me through email on vikram.khaitan@gmail.com and also visit my website www.khaitanvikram.com. Follow me on my Author Central page on Amazon to stay in touch with my next books.

Please watch out for my other publications on Amazon Central. I shall continue to serve you with my writing. Hope to stay connected.

Instagram: https://www.instagram.com/bookwriter_vikram/

Facebook: https://www.facebook.com/vikram.khaitan

YouTube: https://www.youtube.com/c/SipnTalkwithVikram

Website: https://www.khaitanvikram.com

GRATITUDE

I owe this book to role model and hero, Lord Krishna whose teachings in life gave me an opportunity to learn how to recognize my inner-self and enabled me to confront and conquer my inner weaknesses.

I bow to my parents, elders, Gurus, teachers, mentors, guides, friends, prominent personalities—my role models, who have helped shape me as the individual I am; and for the insights I have gained from them about life, that have enabled me to write.

I am grateful to my wife and children who bore with patience, my long absence from their company as I was compiling this book in solitude.

I also express gratitude to each person and organizations who have preserved the essence of the Bhagavad Gita and have spread its teachings across the world.

I express gratitude to Mr.Ashis Mukherjee for writing a foreword for this book and also for giving it critic's review rating.

I express gratitude to Dr.K.R.S.Nair for writing a foreword for this book and suggesting appropriate corrections to make it flawless.

I express deep gratitude to my readers who showered their love and appreciation for all my works and made all 4 books international bestsellers on Amazon. Dear readers, your support and encouragement has given me the energy and inspiration to continue writing with absolute commitment.

ABOUT THE AUTHOR

Vikram Khaitan is an author, mentor, creator and public speaker. He is a seeker and philosopher who looks beyond the existing challenges to find solutions for the future. His keen sense of observation and comprehension of life makes him look at things differently. He brings across solutions to help improve life, develop a positive attitude, enhance the thought process, improve career, money & finance, health, relationships and the mind.

Vikram is a four times #1 international bestselling author on Amazon with three successful books in a row.

a) The Secrets To A Magical Life
b) How To Grow Rich & Become Wealthy
c) Master The Art Of Ageing Gracefully
d) Seeds of Advice To Sail Through Hard Times

He is also a creator on YouTube with his unique show "Sip n Talk with Vikram" where he brings out interesting stories out of people and their experiences through one to one interviews and also presents lovely book reviews in his own inimitable style. He also shares practical learning through his unique feature called Lateral Learning.

DISCLAIMER

The content of this book deals with various life skills which got widely accepted and followed across the world, including India. These are repeatedly published by many people and organisations in many ways. The Bhagavad Gita is a universal guide for teaching good values in life. Also, various behavioral scientists, psychologists and thinkers have propounded their theories based on their own learnings as I learnt my own philosophies in life. My perceptions and understanding may coincide with people who share common values with me or contradict with the beliefs of those who disagree with me. There is no intention to endorse someone else's learning as mine because I have sought my own truths and beliefs through my research, practice and experience. Also, I do not intend to hurt the sentiments of anyone, because this is my story as I perceive it to be and we all see the world from our own unique point of view.

THEY SAID IT!

Here are some testimonials about my works.

Book #1: ***The Secrets To A Magical Life***

Soon after its release it became #1 International Bestseller in USA (Amazon.com), Canada (amazon.ca) and Australia (Amazon.com.au) and #1 Hot new release in U.K. (amazon.co.uk). The book has sold across nine countries across the globe.

Here is what my readers said about this book:

1. *"I like how you use examples and illustrative stories to get teaching points across. Makes me think of the way Dr. Srikumar Rao also teaches and writes."* - Ms. Jacqueline Fox–MS-Program Manager, The Rao Institute (via Gmail)

2. *"Amazing insights into how to experience magical life. It focuses on how we can*

improve our lives and be joyful." —Vijay Elhence

3. *"Upon reading this book, I can surely say it's Inspiring, Interesting, allows you to do self-observance & self-improvement and many more.... Author has narrated life's event in very crisp manner that it becomes difficult to keep this book aside once you've started reading it. I loved it because I could link up many events of my life which got overlooked in today's competitive busy life..."* - Adv. Swapnil Modi.

4. *"Situations come in life when life looks like a mess. Feeling comes like we are heading for nowhere everything goes off color. Whenever anyone comes to face such a situation, finding no outlet for worries to drain out, then this book can give you some simple solutions to make yourself feel special once again. For many, this book can be a ray of hope and a true game changer. Writer deserves a big thank for bringing such a meaningful content in such simple words."* —Vijay Bisht

5. *"Powerful Life Mantra! Superb ideas to follow and implement to achieve success in life. The language of the book is simple, with powerful life mantras for success.*

This book will help you train your mind and body to develop the strength of healthy intelligence and enable you to deal with all situations. Highly recommended!"—Ajit Jha

Book #2: **How To Grow Rich And Become Wealthy**

Soon after its release, this book also became #1 International Bestseller in USA (Amazon.com), Canada (amazon.ca) and Australia (Amazon.com.au) and #1 Hot new release in U.K. (amazon.co.uk).

Here is what my readers said about this book:
1. *"A great overview that makes it easy to take action. It's entertaining and takes you step by step, at your own pace, into the complex world of decisions and priorities to make. I look forward to his next book. Great work!"*-Dan Agervig Hansen.

2. "Wealth is the yardstick to know how well one is using one's abilities. Many of the richest persons in the modern era were economically poor. They harnessed the means and found the right mentors to become what they are today. Vikram Khaitan is such a mentor. Through this simple yet very informative and practical book, he guides one by the hand as I felt. It is must read for all age groups as there is no age bar for growth."-Fr.C. George Mary Claret.

3. "The cover itself sets the tone that this book is about creating wealth for yourself as you grow. A very useful book for all those looking for understanding the art of saving from an early age. The suggestions are very doable and help the reader get conscious about the habit of saving for your dusk years. I recommend this book to the readers of all ages to stay happy in your retirement. Great reading."-Virendra Kashyap.

4. "Personal finance is a field about which most of us do not know! In this book, the author takes the reader through a journey towards financial freedom in a step-by-step manner, ensuring none of the important aspect gets missed out. The book develops both the MIND-SET and the SKILL-SET, which are required to grow rich and wealthy. There is a stark difference between being RICH and being WEALTHY, immerse yourself in this piece

of wisdom to unearth the recipe."-Santosh Singh.

5. *"An uninterrupted dialogue with every professional help to manage and grow your finances. A guide with the detailing of book-keeping and providing even formats along with the information that how markets behave is just amazing. A must have for all households."*-Anupama Rawat.

Book #3: **How To Grow Rich And Become Wealthy**

Soon after its release, this book also became #1 International Bestseller in USA (Amazon.com), Canada (amazon.ca) and Australia (Amazon.com.au) and #1 Hot new release in U.K. (amazon.co.uk).

Here is what my readers said about this book:
1. *This book teaches youth how to use life laws in line with modern medical science gifts to learn how to preserve their youth and conserve their energy and resources as they grow older every day. This book is all*

about taking care of yourself. It talks about health, happiness, financial well-being, safety, and every other important aspect of life. This creation is also a small refresher course of the principles of Eastern philosophy. – CA Ram Pawan Kumar

2. *A very systematic compilation of many levels of wisdom. The book prepares a person for years ahead in advance so that one can be you happy enthusiastic and peaceful life till the death. It guides on all fronts like finance, fitness, social and spiritual. All the nuggets of wisdom are spread everywhere in the book. I read the book in one go. It is impossible to stop reading once you start. It must be used as a ready reckoner all the time for self-help by each of us. The book also combines the east and the west wisdom and the ways of living happily. Very decent and smooth writing in simple words is another plus point of the book. Highly recommended. It is a very practical book with many simple but profound tips. - Dr Vikas Dongre.*

3. *Most informative book covering all aspects of Aging! This book provides a comprehensive view on every aspect of aging! Every person irrespective of whether young or old can get valuable, practical solutions to lead a healthy, happy and peaceful life. It indeed enables us to develop sunshine growth for a golden sunset!! – GSK*

4. *Aging is not just about getting old. Everyone is aging by the day. This book is for the young people to prepare for a happy and bright future, as well as for the old to figure out what more to expect from life in the sunset years. The author knows to weave magic with words and has provided practical tips for safeguarding your health, finances, safety and security, which seems to slip as you grow old. Highly recommended. – Gita Ramachandran*

5. *Amazing Book Mr. Vikram Khaitan like your other books. Earlier I thought this is meant for people who are old, however I realised this is meant for everyone especially those who are young. It is to be read by all age category and live your life to the fullest. Thanks for enlightening us in this manner. – Dr.Ravindra Dey*

About my YouTube Channel – Sip n Talk with Vikram

"Vikram sir has asked such immense questions n such great n wonderful answers were given ...totally next level interview... AMAZING!" – Anju Bathla Arora.

"Vikram, love your dignified way of Sip n Talk. Reminds me of AB (Amitabh Bachhan) of KBC (Kaun Banega Crorepati), who makes the guest feel equally big and at ease. Keep it coming. Thanks. – Kishore Gidwani.

"Enjoyed watching this show. Each episode demonstrates the authority Vikram possesses in different genres. – Gita Ramachandran

REFERENCES

https://vedabase.io/en/library

https://medcraveonline.com/MOJYPT/MOJYPT-03-00056.pdf

https://www.theladders.com/career-advice/there-are-three-types-of-arrogance-which-type-do-you-have

https://sintelly.com/articles/there-are-different-types-of-jealousy-and-they-all-damage-your-wellbeing

https://www.aarp.org/home-family/friends-family/info-2019/medical-cure-for-loneliness.html

https://medium.com/s/story/the-three-kinds-of-laziness-81d0127bd738

https://www.stylist.co.uk/long-reads/how-to-deal-with-loneliness-types-emotional-situational-social-chronic/222923#:~:text=Loneliness%20affects%20people%20in%20different,%2C%20social%2C%20situational%20and%20chronic.

https://www.hypnosis-in-london.com/9-types-hopelessness-overcome/

https://www.lifehack.org/articles/productivity/10-types-demotivation-and-how-overcome-them.html

https://www.productiveflourishing.com/how-to-recover-from-10-types-of-demotivation/

https://www.youtube.com/watch?v=tGdsOXZpyWE

https://www.youtube.com/watch?v=1XZa_ouLNiw

https://www.youtube.com/watch?v=DJ71pKKDe1E&t=402s

Amazing short stories: https://www.youtube.com/watch?v=fs28hEwXw_8

https://www.youtube.com/watch?v=9DbvS1_C_kY – Japanese technique

https://www.youtube.com/watch?v=T6vc9oPH4i8

Goodreads.com and Brainyquotes.com for lovely inspirational quotes

Wiki for it's vast treasure of knowledge, without which any knowledge is incomplete.